This book is dedicated to Jamie, you have been my reason for being for your whole life and have made me the proudest mum. Your strength, kindness and compassion never fails to amaze me. Never ever change, keep being you.

Love Mum

INTRODUCTION

In July 1998 I started my dream job, the job I had always wanted to do since I was a very young girl. I joined the Royal Air Force as a Policewoman. Little did I know just how much that job would change my life or shape me into the person that I am now. I have so many memories from that wonderful career, but this book is set after that stage in my life. Although a lot of the people I met during that time have been part of the support network that I have surrounded us with. It's true what they say, friends made in service last a lifetime.

Whilst based at RAF Northolt in London in 2004 I deployed to Basrah, Iraq, on Op Telic. During that deployment I met Chris who was serving in the Army as a chef. What I thought would be a detachment romance blossomed over the following months into something so much bigger and we both fell deeply in love. We used to travel to each other's bases on our time off, I had moved to RAF Marham and Chris was based in Canterbury with the 5 Scots. It wasn't easy all the time, but we made it work and we married in July 2006. We chose to live at Marham because at the time I worked night shifts.

Jamie (J) arrived in March 2008 to complete our family, we had no idea then what a special young man he would turn out to be, but he was and is very much loved. Chris unfortunately deployed to Afghan when J was just 8 days old, as hard as that was, we knew it was part of our lives in the forces.

In the July of 2009 Chris came home and told me that he was posted to Germany in the October. This threw our world upside down; in my current job I had no chance of being posted to Germany and I had no idea if I would get a quick release. After lots of long discussions and pleading on my part with my chain of command they agreed to sign the paperwork, so the Smalls were off on a new adventure. This was a huge upheaval for me, I loved my job, and it was part of my identity, but I felt it was so important to keep our family together. Forces partners worldwide give up so much to keep our families together and I think that is often forgotten.

Chris changed after his last tour of Afghan and when he returned in the March of 2012, he wasn't the same person I had said goodbye to seven months previously. Following this, whilst Chris was in Kenya the chance to take redundancy came, he jumped at it, he said he wanted us all to have a normal life. We returned back to the UK in August 2013 and found ourselves in Harrogate although Chris had requested Woodbridge so we could be close to family.

Unfortunately, Chris struggled with life outside of the Army, not in regard to finding a job but he was trying to find what he had in the Army and that just doesn't exist on the outside. He was drinking more, spending money we didn't have, taking out loans and not paying them back, gambling and the final straw seeing other women. Both myself and J had been walking on eggshells since Chris had returned from Afghan over two years before and although I believe that tour changed him, I think it was just the catalyst. You can't serve for 21 years, deploy to every conflict during that time, sometimes numerous times and it not affect you in some way.

Walking away from our marriage in June 2015 was one of the hardest things I've ever done but it was something I had to do for my own mental wellbeing and through that J's mental wellbeing. By staying together, we would have slowly destroyed each other, Chris was no longer the man I had fallen in love with, and he was showing a side that I hadn't known existed. Before we left Chris was violent towards me in front of J, I knew then that I had made the right decision and that J could not be brought up in that environment. I didn't leave because I didn't love Chris, I left because it was no longer possible to live with him.

Now I know it was all part of a much bigger picture but before we split, I begged Chris to get help, he wouldn't entertain that at all, his pride was standing in the way. Until he admitted that he needed help I was hitting my head against a brick wall, I could see he was struggling and so could others but Chris either couldn't or wouldn't. After we split up Chris had another female in his life who was living with him on and off, having seen the state of the house in the days after Chris's death all the signs were there of what was going on. It angers me that someone who said they loved him chose to ignore all the obvious signs of Mental Health problems and in some ways was enabling it to her benefit. Chris was told by this person that if he asked for help, he would look weak. He told me this in the last contact we ever had with each other and it's something that haunts me to this day.

This story picks up from the day we got the devastating news about Chris, I talk about the highs and lows of our life since. This is our story, it's our feelings and how we've learnt to live with a life changing tragedy. I hope it makes people realise how suicide affects so many different people and how it forever alters those closest to the person who's lost.

THE PHONECALL

On Tuesday 29th November 2016 the day started just like any other day. I had a day off from my new job as a Health Care Assistant on the Stroke ward in Ipswich Hospital and J had been at school. J and I were sitting on the sofa watching TV, relaxing before I dropped him at my parents as I was due in work the next day. I received a Facebook message from Chris's stepbrother Graham asking for my mobile number. I had a sinking feeling in my stomach because we always communicated over social media so the fact that he wanted to speak to me meant that something was wrong. This worried me and I didn't know if I wanted to hear what he had to say. I thought that maybe something had happened to Chris's dad, John, we had maintained a relationship with him since Chris and I separated, and Graham knew that we were close. I never imagined he would be telling me what he did though. A few minutes later my mobile rang, and Graham said he had some bad news, at this point I told J I was nipping outside and asked Graham to wait a second. We lived in a first floor flat then, so I went downstairs and out the front, I remember that it was raining and cold because I had no coat on and it hit me as soon as I walked out. I lit a cigarette and asked Graham what had happened, I had an awful, nervous feeling in my stomach because I knew whatever he said was going to affect us, it had to be big otherwise he wouldn't have rung us. Nothing prepared me for what he said next, he said that Chris had died and that he had taken his own life. I instantly felt numb but still the tears came straight away, this couldn't be true, not Chris, I thought I must have heard wrong. I made no attempt to wipe the tears away and all I could say was, 'why?' This was a question that Graham couldn't answer and still to this day we can't answer fully. Looking back, I feel so bad for Graham, what an horrendous phone call to make and then he spent the rest of the call comforting me when he must have been hurting himself as well. Him and Chris had always had a good relationship and although they didn't talk all the time, they were very close.

In that very moment my whole world came crashing down around me and although Chris and I were separated he was J's dad and for that reason I would always love him. Also, I was still very much in love with the man that I had married although I knew that Chris would never have been that person again, you can't turn your feelings on and off though. It suddenly hit me that sitting inside on the sofa was our 8-year-old son and I was going to have to find the words to tell him what had happened. I knew however I put it then I was going to break his heart and nothing I said or did would be able to stop the hurt. I will never hide the fact that the thought of telling J absolutely terrified me, no one wants to hurt the person closest to them but there was no way of breaking this news without doing that. I had never lied to him, and I certainly wasn't going to start with something as big as this. I knew that I had to put my own feelings to one side and try and find the strength from somewhere. I didn't feel strong, my legs were like jelly, my hands were shaking, and I couldn't stop crying, but that young, innocent, wonderful young boy sat inside needed his mum. I was going to have to step up and be stronger than I'd ever been. I took a deep breath and started to walk up the stairs back inside. So many thoughts were going through my head in that very short journey, how was I going to tell J, how was he going to take it, would he even understand? There was one thing that I was certain of though and that was that our lives had changed forever.

I wiped my eyes although it had no effect as the tears were still sneaking out of the corner of them and walked back in the flat. As I approached J, he looked at me with worry in his young eyes and I knew from his face that he knew something was wrong. He is so switched on to other people's feelings and the very fact that I went outside to speak to Uncle Graham spoke volumes to him. I sat on the sofa next to him and pulled him onto my lap, I took a deep breath and tried to control my voice and my feelings, not an easy task. I then said the hardest words I've ever said or will have to say, 'I'm so so very sorry sweetheart but daddy has died'. Straight away he started to cry and not normal crying but the huge sobs where you struggle to catch your breath. I put my arms round him as tight as I could and he sobbed into my shoulder, tears were falling from my face, and I made no attempt to stop them. My heart was breaking, not just hurting it felt someone was sticking knives into it, all I could see was the pain I had just caused him, and I thought that very moment was going to destroy me. It was probably the lowest I felt during this whole period, and I was lost, there was nothing I could do to help J and I could feel myself falling rapidly. To see the person, you love the most in the world heart broken and know there is nothing you can do to stop it is truly soul destroying. I didn't know what to do to try and ease his pain so I just cuddled him, I held him as close to me as I could hoping that he could feel all the love I have for him.

We sat like that for a while and then I phoned my parents, my mum was already on her way to us because Chris's half-brother had phoned my parents as they didn't have my number. When Chris and I had separated we lost contact with some of Chris's family due to various reasons. Whilst we were waiting for my mum Jamie asked how his dad had died, this was a pivotal point in this journey, I could lie and say a common reason for it, or I could tell the truth and introduce J to a whole new world. I had a split second to make one of the most important decisions of my life and if I made the wrong one it could further destroy our lives.

I made the choice that I thought was right at the time and to this day I stand by that decision. I didn't want J to think a bad person had hurt his dad and I also knew that if I lied then eventually J would find out the truth and that could destroy the bond we have. Explaining Mental Health to an 8-year-old is very difficult and I had to do it in a way that he could not only understand but also process. Pulling J into my arms again and kissing the top of his head I told him that daddy had been very very sad and that his heart and head were hurting, and he'd done something to help ease the pain, but it had been very dangerous and had meant that it had stopped his pain forever. I'm sure people have their own ideas on how I should have explained this, but hindsight is a wonderful thing and explaining suicide to an adult is difficult let alone to an 8-year-old who had never even heard the word before. In fact, I've even been told by some people that I shouldn't have told him it was suicide but that's something I would never have done. Mental health is not something to be ashamed off and I didn't want Jamie to find out from another source. I'm not ashamed of the fact that Chris took his own life, I'm very sad that he felt this was the only way to solve his problems and angry that those around him ignored what were obvious signs.

When my mum arrived, she didn't know we already knew what had happened so was shocked to see the scene in front of her. She said that she was taking us both back to theirs as they didn't want us to be alone. I started to close off at that time, this had to be about J, and I had to be at my strongest. I felt that I couldn't cry in front of him because it would upset him, so I did the typical English thing and put on a stiff upper lip. That was something that I did regret a while down the journey but again it was what I thought was right at the time. For me though making it all about J was what I needed to do to stay strong, if I thought about what I needed I knew that I would break. I had to concentrate on something, to keep my mind busy and not allow myself too much time to think. I thought that thinking too much would be dangerous because I thought it would cause me to breakdown.

I phoned work that night to say I wouldn't be on shift the next day and they were amazing considering I hadn't even worked there for 2 weeks. This is a shout out to all that work on Shotley Stroke Ward, Ipswich Hospital, you've all been there for me since the start of this journey and your support has been invaluable. I also text my best friend Gail as I didn't think I could face talking to anyone, even her (we've been best friends since the age of 11). The amazing friend that she is, she didn't text back; she rang because as best friends do, she knew that I needed to talk. Gail and her family have been there for me and J through thick and thin and are no longer friends they are family.

J slept with me that night on my parent's sofa bed and he cried himself to sleep wrapped in my arms. When J had fallen into a semi deep sleep, I allowed myself to cry and I mean really cry, I felt like my heart was breaking in two. I don't think I've cried like that since, apart from maybe at the funeral, sobbing into my pillow not being able to believe what had happened. Why had Chris done this? I knew he was struggling but I had told him I would always be there for him, why hadn't he phoned me or text me? I relived so many memories that night, happy memories and I could see Chris in front of me laughing and giving me one of his winning smiles. I remembered the man that I had fallen in love with, the laughter we had shared, all the good times. Memories popped into my mind that I thought I had forgotten, this just made me cry more though knowing that I would never see his face again or hear him laugh. Whilst laying there I text my other best mate Vicki to tell her, I wasn't expecting a response because it was so late and, in the morning, she text me back and we arranged to talk in a day or two when my head was a bit straighter. Like Gail, Vicki has been there for us 24/7 and has let me unburden myself many a time. These two ladies have played such an important part in this journey, and they don't give themselves enough credit, you are not only there for the good times but also the bad, true friendship.

 I will never ever forget that night due to many reasons, I had lost the man that I once loved more than life itself and I had also watched our sons heart break in front of my eyes. Neither of us got much proper sleep that night and we both got up in the morning like we'd not slept in weeks. I felt like I'd been drinking the previous night, tired, a stinking headache and feeling like I would never smile again. We had to get up though and face whatever the day threw at us, we hadn't died and for us life had to go on. As emotional and horrendous as that night was though it strengthened an already awesome bond between me and J. He realised that night that I will always be honest with him and that whatever happens we will face it together and as a team. That's still true today, we face everything as a team and J knows without a doubt that I've got his back and I know that he has got mine.

The Following Days

On the Wednesday morning I made the decision for J to go to school, I wanted him to keep his routine, I had the feeling that was going to be important, and I also wanted him to be surrounded by friends. I was also scared that if he didn't go then, he would struggle when he needed to go back. When I was walking him to school, he asked who had found daddy, I told him the police had broken in and tried to help him. He thought about that for a few minutes and then asked if the police would make daddy phone him and tell him off for not seeing him. My heart sank and we stopped walking, I crouched to his level and said do you remember when Kai (our GSD) died, and he went to heaven where he could go through the rubbish bins and chase cats? J said yes and that Kai watches over us wherever we are, he paused and said is that where daddy is? I nodded and gave him the biggest hug, I'm still not sure that he actually processed it at that point, but he had some understanding. He seemed to find a bit of peace that daddy was with Kai so that neither of them would be alone. I watched him closely during that walk to school and I could see that he was trying to process things. When we walked through the school gates, he looked up at me and said, 'I love you mummy', how I didn't break down there and then I don't know. I looked him straight in the eyes and said, 'I will always love you and I couldn't be prouder of you then I am right now'.

We walked through the main doors, and I spoke to the secretary, Shelly and asked if I could speak to a teacher, she took one look at J's red eyes took him off to breakfast club and found me a senior teacher. After I spoke to him, I went to find J, he was sat in a classroom with his teacher and TA. J has always loved school and is so sociable and I mentioned this when I had a chat with them and they agreed that Jamie being in school was good for him, he was able to choose one friend and they spent the day together. He chose his mate Cam, and I knew that even if J wasn't smiling by the end of the day, it would at least help to keep his mind occupied. The SENCO spoke to me before I left that morning and had already started putting things in place for J. You hear horror stories all the time about schools not being supportive through trauma but Wickham Market Primary Schools support of J during this period went above and beyond. From the head teacher to the teachers and TA's, the secretary and the dinner ladies, all of them were fantastic and made the next few weeks a lot easier for J. It was so important that J felt safe in school, and it was also important that I trusted the school to protect and help me, I wasn't disappointed at all.

After leaving J there and on the way home from school I started making phone calls to Chris's main friends because I didn't want them to hear about his death on social media. I knew it wouldn't be long before people heard on the grapevine and started posting things and no one should find out that way. I phoned Dave and Chris Jubb first; we had been in Germany with them and were both still extremely close to them. Telling people was so hard because you can't beat around the bush, and you just have to say it. Every time I told someone it broke my heart, and it was like I was reliving being told for the first time every time. I knew each time I dialled a number that I was going to be hurting someone and at that moment I hated myself. All I seemed to be doing was causing others so much pain and that was really starting to affect me. Dave took it hard as you can imagine, him and Chris had been very close, but every time Dave reached out to him Chris pushed him away. As soon as I said the words to him the phone went silent and his wife came on the phone, I could hear the devastation in her voice, and I could hear Dave in the background. I then phoned Locky who Chris had met and become really good friends with early in his career. I don't think he knew what to say and was more concerned about me and J which is still the case to this day. Locky has become an amazing friend over the years and although we don't speak often, I know that he's always there for us both. It amazes me how many of Chris's friends have taken on the role of protecting us, they never impose on us, but we know that they are there which is so important and will never be forgotten. That of course works both ways, I hope that those who have been there for us know that I will always be there for them if they ever need me.

When I got back to my parents, I knew that I had so many things to sort out, I had to phone the Police in Bishop Auckland, the military pensions to stop Chris's pension and I also had to contact Chris's mum and I knew that wasn't going to be an easy phone call. That was the call I was most worried about and actually put it off for as long as I could. I knew she knew about Chris so I wasn't hiding anything, but I was nervous over what sort of reaction I would get.

I phoned the Police first and spoke to DS Graham Lowe who was in charge of Chris's case. We had a long chat, and he was both professional and caring. As it turned out he was an ex RMP, so we had the natural feeling of being at ease that you have with fellow Veterans. I actually nominated him for a WOW award a couple of months later for all the support he gave us which he won. Graham talked me through what I needed to do next including contacting the coroner as Chris still needed to be officially ID'd. I volunteered to do this as although I knew it would be extremely difficult, I didn't want his parents to see him like that, no parent deserves to go through something like that.

I spoke to the coroner and arranged to view Chris on the Friday, it also meant that I could go to the house we had shared and get some things that would mean something to J and be a way of remembering his dad.

I knew then I couldn't put off contacting Christine (Chris's mum) anymore, this was going to be a difficult phone call for numerous reasons. Firstly, she had just lost her son through horrendous circumstances and our relationship had broken down completely when Chris and I separated. I put my pride to one side for the next few months and tried to build a relationship. Due to reasons that I am not going into the relationship broke down a couple of months after the funeral and we now have no contact. It's a shame that she won't see J grow up but sometimes relationships cannot be saved. Thankfully though we still have a relationship with Chris's Uncles, Aunts, cousins, his stepbrother and dad.

The next difficult phone call I needed to make was to Chris's dad John. Since moving back to Suffolk, myself and J had built a good relationship with him, and he plays a part in J's life. John never took sides when Chris and I separated, and it was important to him to be in J's life. When Chris died John was on holiday in Malta, the last thing I wanted to do was tell him over the phone what had happened but there was also a chance again that he would see something on social media, and I didn't want that. I bit the bullet and rang, he was shocked to hear my voice but started to tell me about his holiday, I had to cut him short and tell him that I had bad news. I asked him if he was sat down and if he was with his friends and yet again, I had to say those words that Chris was dead. Whatever he thought I was going to say I could tell it definitely wasn't that. Again, I felt useless, there was nothing I could say to make it better, I'd just told him that his only child had died and there is no way of making that sound any less painful. We spoke for a bit longer and John said that he would be home late on that Friday. We arranged for me to phone again when he was home and arrange to meet. We then hung up with me feeling again like I had destroyed someone's life and there was nothing I could do about it. This is the thing with suicide, it affects so many people afterwards, it's a true ripple effect. Already so many people's lives had been changed because we had lost Chris and we were only a couple of days into our journey.

My mum and I drove to Coundon, Bishop Auckland in the early hours on the Friday morning, it was a long emotional drive knowing what I had ahead of me both seeing Chris and seeing the house that we had both fallen in love with. We arrived at around 10 o'clock after having stopped at the Police station to get the keys and some of Chris's personal belongings and as we pulled up the neighbours came out and invited us in for a brew which was very much appreciated. Whilst I was drinking mine mum went into the house to make sure there was nothing to upset me. Unfortunately, when the Police had broken in there was some damage to the door. Mum didn't realise this, unlocked it and pushed and the whole door fell inwards. That at least lightened the moment somewhat and I started to laugh, that would be the last time I laughed that day, that laughter soon turned to tears.

The first thing I noticed when I walked in the door was the mess, not just untidy but rubbish and dirt, it was filthy, like something you've never seen in your life. Just after we walked in the Landlords mum rang the bell and came in to give her condolences, I had got to know her whilst I was living there and just seeing the sympathy in her face was enough to reduce me to tears. She gave me a big hug and said nothing, no words were needed at that point. Whilst she was there, I found the eviction notice, Chris hadn't paid his rent for over 6 months, and he was due to leave the house in the following January. She arranged for the landlord to ring me and considering how out of pocket he was he was so respectful. I hope he felt no guilt from this, if you don't pay your bills that there are consequences, he had been extremely patient with Chris and gave him so many chances to sort it out. Even after we left that day, he found more things that he thought Jamie would like and put them to one side for us. I told him to sell the furniture to try and recoup some of his money, but he refused and gave it to charity. That alone says an awful lot about what sort of person he is.

Whilst I was sorting through the mess trying to find things for J mum made a start on tidying up. There was no way I could hand it back to the landlord in the state it was but there's also no way I can put into words what a state it was in. Before we left, we filled numerous large bin bags, we found beer cans both empty and half drunk, overflowing ashtrays, these were in every room including the bathroom, mouldy food amongst many other things. There was a carton of half empty orange juice under his bed that had been there so long that it was full of mould and the carton was starting to expand. The thought that Chris was living like that broke my heart, but it also made me angry that he was pretty much living with someone, and she thought that was normal. I managed to get items for J that he could either display or put in a memory box, the most important of which were Chris's medals. Chris was a huge Liverpool fan which he passed on to J, so I also brought home lots of his Liverpool memorabilia and pictures of the three of us which were still up all round the house.

Whilst we were there, I found a box of post, most of which was unopened but what had been opened were final demands, letters from bailiffs or fines that were increasing every time they were ignored. Scattered all around the house were brand new items from catalogues still in their packaging, a new laptop, sofa and TV. Whilst going through the post it was obvious that no payments had been made on any of these items. Behaviour like this is one of the signs of Mental Health issues but it seems those that were supposed to be closest to Chris thought that it was normal behaviour. After I had read through all the bills etc. it became clear that Chris was in debt of upwards of £50,000. This didn't include the loan he had taken out that his mum guaranteed and consequently she had to repay. I'm sure that many more letters would arrive after we left, and it was devastating to think of the problems Chris had caused himself just to give a certain impression to the outside world. Speaking to the neighbours they said that the curtains and windows hadn't been opened in months, I can only guess that was to give the impression that he wasn't in. That unfortunately is the sort of world we live in today. A world where more importance is put on material items then what a person can bring to someone's life.

I left our dream house for the last time, knowing in my heart I would never return to the village as it was far too painful. We drove to Darlington and met with the coroner who then took me to Chris. To see the man that you had such high hopes for and imagined a long happy life with laid out in a mortuary is devastating. He didn't look like Chris, although I would know him anywhere, he had lost so much weight and his face was sunken, not my

Chris at all. Seeing him laying there like that was surreal and as I was getting more emotional it became too much and I had to leave the room to be sick. I spent a bit of time trying to sort his hair because it wasn't right at all, and he always used to make sure it was done. The thing that really shocked me was that he hadn't been shaving, Chris was the type of man that would move mountains if it meant he could have his daily shave. I think maybe he grew a beard to try and hide the fact that he had lost so much weight in his face but anyone that knew him would have noticed. I spent a bit of time with him, mainly having words which I hope to God he heard but, I also told him that I loved him and that he had taken a piece of my heart with him. I told him how devastated both myself and J were and that our lives would never be the same again. I told him I would make sure that J would never forget him and that we would make him proud. Before saying my final goodbye, I asked him to always keep me and Jamie safe and to save me a seat at the elite bar for when we meet again. During these last few minutes with him I couldn't even hold his hand, so I just placed mine on top of his, then I stroked his face like I always used to and kissed him on the forehead and left him. Tears were streaming from my face; my stomach was in my mouth and my heart was breaking. How was it possible that the man I loved, the man who was so full of laughter and life was laying like this in front of me, still with the noose around his neck. What had gone so wrong that he chose a permanent end to temporary problems, if I couldn't understand it then how was J going to?

The journey home was strange, it was pouring with rain which matched my mood and I spent much of the time looking out of the window with so many questions going through my mind. When we got back to my parents and I saw J we gave each other the biggest hug, he was what I needed right in that moment, and I was what he needed. I put the things I'd gotten for J in my car; we got in and drove back to ours. I knew then that we had to go home and start living our lives again however hard that would be. The easy option would have been to stay at mum and dads for a bit longer, but I knew the longer we stayed the harder it would be to leave. It was time to start the next part of our journey however hard that was going to be.

I will never ever forget what my parents did for us after Chris's death and what they still do now. The relationship that they have with J is paramount to him getting through this and the support they give me on a daily basis is nothing short of amazing. We are truly blessed to have them in our lives. I honestly don't think they know just how much we love them or how much we appreciate every last thing they do for us. Mum and Dad, we love you and thank you. I don't think we tell the people around us how we feel enough but what I've learnt from this is how fragile life is. Please take every opportunity to tell those you love how you feel.

The Following Weeks

So much needed sorting over the next few weeks and my head felt like a bomb waiting to go off constantly. I was being pulled in all directions, the news had gone viral on Facebook, and I was suddenly hearing off people that I hadn't spoken to in months, even years in some cases, so many people were asking when the funeral would be and wanting answers that I just couldn't give. I'm sure a lot of people didn't mean anything by it, but it felt like they were all getting at me and to top it off some people took it upon themselves to tell me exactly how they felt about people who took their own lives, that hurt me more than I've ever admitted. We are all entitled to our own opinion but in some circumstances it's maybe best not to voice them. Telling me that they thought my husband was a coward and selfish days after he had died was just cruel. You would be amazed by how damaging comments like this are, especially when they fester in your mind. I hope those people never find themselves battling with such horrendous demons or find themselves so low that they think suicide is the only way out. In amongst all of this I was trying to get J through each day and to a certain degree myself as well.

I contacted SSAFA because I had worked alongside them when I was in the RAF. They returned my phone call within 24 hours, and I was put in touch with a local caseworker, Sue who would turn out to be a godsend. We arranged a convenient time to meet up and when she came round, she sat down and listened to me. I mean really listened, no interruptions, no talking over me, she just let me get everything off my chest. She let me cry, talk and vent and most importantly she didn't judge Chris. Sue went through all the paperwork with me and was going to try and get funding from forces charities for the funeral because the cost of that had put the fear of God into me and I had no idea where I would find the money. Just one of the many things that people forget about when someone dies.

She didn't disappoint and within a matter of weeks we had enough money to pay for the funeral that Chris had always said he wanted. Chris was going to be brought back from Durham to Colchester as that's where he had grown up and it was only right that that was where he was laid to rest. As well as that Sue gained us a grant to buy Jamie a new wardrobe which had just collapsed and caused me to have a major melt down, it's amazing that what seems like a small issue causes the biggest reaction. Still to this day we spend time with Sue, and we consider her a friend for life. I will speak more about SSAFA later in the book.

Throughout the time between Chris dying and his funeral I was driving to and from Colchester on my days off in between school drop off and pickups trying to finalise plans. Because of the time of year and it being so close to Christmas then we had quite a gap before the funeral because I didn't want it over the Christmas period. Through the year there are plenty of anniversaries where we remember Chris, I was adamant I didn't want one of them to be the Christmas period, Chris loved Christmas and I wanted that to be kept as a happy memory.

This made the Christmas period quite difficult because we had to function as normally as possible but also have the fear of the funeral hanging over us. Christmas did happen though and as difficult as it was to get into the spirit, I knew I had to. I had an 8-year-old who still believed in Santa and all the magic associated with that period and I was determined to make it special for him. I could either let him down and us both be miserable, or I could put a smile on my face and try to make it his best Christmas yet. I chose the second option as I'm sure any parent would, I won't tell you it was easy because it was far from that, both J and I had our moments over the holidays, but we survived, and I like to think that J found some enjoyment in it.

We spent the day with my parents and although it was quiet, we were surrounded by people who love us and that was exactly what we needed to get through it. I believe that J had a good time over the holidays though and managed to get in the spirit, it may have helped that Santa had been very good to him. More importantly though J smiled again during that period and I'm talking a proper smile that reached his eyes. To see his young face light up like that and for him not to look like he was carrying the weight of the world on his shoulders was amazing. That was the best Christmas present I could receive because he hadn't smiled like that since we had heard the news. They say the first of everything is the worst and I can honestly say that never a truer word has been spoken.

New Year was a bit easier for us because it's never been something we've made a bit thing off. J wanted to be with me that night with was becoming something of a regular occurrence, I'll admit I didn't mind because it was a comfort knowing he was close. We got in our pyjamas early, made hot chocolates and snuggled in bed watching a movie. We both dropped off way before midnight. To me the only thing the New Year meant to me was the funeral and I would have done anything to have delayed that.

J went back to school after the holidays excited to see his friends but still holding himself back a bit, not the confident, happy boy he used to be. He was very clingy during this period and would have melt downs if I was late home from work or if our routine changed. I quickly learnt that a key to his recovery would involve me reassuring him at every opportunity that I could. He used to ask me to promise him that I wouldn't die, I couldn't do that but what I could do and still do today is promise him that I won't leave him on purpose. At 8 J was far too young for me to discuss mental health in depth with him but I did keep mentioning that his dad didn't want to leave him and that his dad had been ill when he died. I also said that when J is older, I will sit down, and I'll tell him everything and answer any questions he's got.

It did J the world of good being at school surrounded by friends, the vast majority of kids were fantastic and if J said he didn't want to discuss it then they went along with that. The odd few took the opportunity to use it against him, but the teachers were quick to nip it in the bud and no big problems arose for him around that time, that however did change over the next couple of years. J has always enjoyed school, so it was fantastic that it was still able to be a safe place for him. It also gave him something to focus on and help to clear his mind of his dad, although he will always be there in his mind J needed to be able to think about different things and to be a child. If all he got from being at school during that period was running round with his mates at break and dinner, then that was more than enough.

He also did gymnastics during this time which he loved, and he had made a good friend there Jack. Neither of them does the sport anymore but they have kept in touch and help each other when times are hard. I also formed a close bond with Jack's mum Natalia and hope she knows that if she ever needs anything I'll always be there. I still miss the laughs we used to have on that balcony week in and week out.

The Funeral

The funeral was something I'd thought about so many times when Chris was serving so I knew his wishes which I think made it that bit easier in the fact that I already knew what was needed. It wasn't something however that I thought I would have to organise so soon after he left the Army. It was held on 9th Jan 2017 at Colchester Crematorium, it was important that Chris was brought home to where he was born. Chris was a huge Liverpool fan, and his first wish was that 'you'll never walk alone' would be the song that the curtains closed to, I knew he would never forgive me if that didn't happen so that was the first thing I organised. I'll always find it ironic that his life ended in the way it did, yet we said goodbye to him with that song, if he had listened to that song closely maybe he would have remembered that people did care about him. His second wish was that he didn't want people in dark suits, he wanted a bit of colour and for people to wear sports shirts, preferably football or rugby. Although if people were still serving, I asked for them to wear uniform because although I didn't want a full military service it was important to respect the fact that Chris had served. For the second time in my life Chris managed to get me in a Liverpool shirt, being a staunch Ipswich fan that came hard, I would have done anything for him at that time though. I got the last word though and I had Chris dressed in an Ipswich shirt, I know he would have taken it in the way it was meant, it would have created one of his cheeky grins and it was a true example of how our relationship used to be before the black dog started to take a hold of Chris.

When Chris arrived at the crematorium with the Union Flag draped over his coffin, I felt like I couldn't breathe, like someone had squeezed all the air out of my lungs. I remember one of Chris's friends saying to me 'I can't believe he's in there' and that summed up what I was thinking. I had asked 6 of his forces friends to act as pall bearers and I can't even begin to realise how hard that was for them. On Chris's behalf though I thank them, it meant a huge amount that they agreed to do it. The last time I had walked up an aisle Chris was stood there waiting for me, not this time though. As a 38-year-old I am following my husband's coffin up the aisle, the moment where I had to say goodbye was coming ever closer. I held my head up high walking behind him, there were tears, but I think I did Chris and myself proud in that moment, I'm sure he would have given me a sign if I hadn't.

As a huge U2 fan I knew that I had to get one of their songs into the service so when he was carried into the crematorium we played 'With or without you'. This may seem like a strange choice, but it was one of his favourites and also one of the songs I enjoy. A military Padre conducted the service and did a fantastic job, he was so respectful but also managed to bring a bit of humour to what he was saying which I know Chris would have appreciated, I know I certainly did. The one thing Chris had never mentioned was the song of reflection and I found it so hard to choose one until one of Chris's oldest friends Emma said to me to choose something that meant something to us both. She also said that whatever I chose would be right and no one would question it which made it easier. I chose our wedding song 'Only one road' by Celine Dion, it certainly made people reflect especially me and for the first time in weeks I sobbed my heart out. My mum put her arm round me and pulled me close and a good friend who was sitting behind me put her hand on my shoulder. Both of those actions meant the absolute world to me, it meant I wasn't alone, although I certainly felt like I was.

My heart didn't just break at the funeral it felt like someone had ripped it out and stamped on it. I think it was at the funeral that it finally sank in that Chris was gone, he wasn't coming back, we'd never speak to him again and we'd never hear that cheeky laugh. The realisation of that hit me full force in the face like a ton of bricks. That day I went through every single emotion, including anger when some people tried to make it all about them. There is a time and a place for grudges and a funeral certainly isn't one of them. I thought the funeral would give me a release and in some ways it did, that was the day I didn't try and be brave, I just let the emotions flow straight over me. As strange as that sounds, I felt an awful lot better for having done that.

Throughout the funeral I sat in the front row, right in front of the picture of Chris on a stand and I just looked at him for the whole service. So many things were going through my head, when we met, when we married, when J was born, all of them happy memories. Those memories made me smile and then I felt guilty for smiling, it didn't mean I was happy though it just meant they were happy memories. Still though the loudest question in my head was what if? Should I have gone back to him when he asked, should I have insisted on contact and what if I'd phoned him that weekend. I knew deep down that none of these things would have changed the outcome and that at some point or another we would have been in this living hell, it may have just been delayed. I looked straight into Chris's eyes begging for him to be real and not just a photo and I knew then that I'd been kidding myself. I did still love Chris and more importantly I had forgiven him for everything that had passed between us. At that moment it was like a huge weight had been lifted from my shoulders.

It was wonderful to be surrounded by our friends for that afternoon because like me they knew the real Chris, not the show that he put on for certain people. J didn't attend the funeral through his own choice, a choice that has never been regretted by him. Our friends however wrote in a memories book for him which has been of huge comfort to him ever since, it shows that his dad was loved by those who knew him and that's very important for him. It was also nice to see members of Chris's family that I hadn't seen in years, we are still in contact with them now and it's lovely for J to know that side of the family although Covid has somewhat delayed meeting up for now.

The wake was held in a social club which wasn't what I would have wanted ideally but some things you just don't have a say in. Chris was a big drinker, most of the time he enjoyed it or relied on it too much and was always the life and soul of any party and I honestly believe that's what he would have wanted for his wake. Both of Chris's brothers said a few words and I said a thank you from me and J for all the support we had received. Quite a few pints were raised to Chris, and I know he would have been looking down at us all smiling for that, I'm not sure he would have been thrilled with the location though.

The Padre said whilst he was talking that the period leading up to the funeral is made bearable because you have something to focus on and so many things to organise but it's the period after that's the hardest because other people go back to their lives whereas that's when the real grieving started for me. Our lives had to go on, we hadn't died but once the funeral was over, I had lost my main focus, the thing that had kept me busy when in those first few weeks. 90% of the messages from people stopped, those closest to me and J obviously stayed in touch, but it seemed that people thought now the funeral was over then the grieving would stop, they were so wrong, the grief was only just starting, now I had the time to over think things. The one thing that I didn't want so I had to find something else to concentrate on.

SSAFA The Forces Charity

I don't often write reviews on companies or products but one day whilst browsing through Facebook I was looking at SSAFA page and I thought I would leave a review. Never did I think that by writing a few sentences our lives would change so much. Although in my mind they deserved so much more but I hoped this would go some way to showing them how much we appreciated what they did. Not long after I received a message from their head office asking if I would be happy to tell our story, well this was perfect, not only a chance to do something for them but also a chance to get our story out there, a chance to help others. Although I wasn't sure that anyone would actually be interested in what I had to say. I don't often admit that I'm wrong but boy was I wrong with that thought. It seemed people were interested in what I had to say, and that people did want to hear our journey. This was such an amazing feeling; Chris's death wasn't going to be in vain and we could use our experience to help others. This put us on a whole new direction in our journey and in our lives.

I sent them a brief outline of our story and they arranged for a photographer to come to ours to get some pictures of me and J. What a day that was, J absolutely loved being in front of the camera and completely came into his own, definitely more comfortable than his mum. The photographer was amazing with him and worked wonders with him, it was fantastic to watch them building a bond throughout the day and the photos only proved what a wonderful job he had done. Both of us truly smiled that day and not forced smiles but real natural ones, ones that come easily. It had been a long time since I had seen J really smile like that and in such a natural scenario. In turn it helped to produce a huge smile on my face. The photos really showed off our bond and how much love we have for each other, and they are something that I will treasure for the rest of my life. Some of them can still be seen scattered around our flat to this day.

We then started to see ourselves and our story appearing in the SSAFA magazine, on the website and the Suffolk branch has a blown-up picture of us on the display on their van (my worst nightmare but J loves it). Through SSAFA I was asked to do an interview for our local radio station and the local TV news in the lead up to Armistice Day. These were so hard to do because not only is Remembrance weekend very difficult but it's also so very close to the anniversary. Both were very emotional interviews and I struggled to hold it together, in fact on the TV I had a few tears, but I think I still managed to come across quite well. An important thing to say here though is that I'm not ashamed that I broke down, it was still so raw and such an emotive subject, we should never be ashamed of showing our feelings. I'm so glad I did them though the response to both was fantastic, not just towards me but it was getting SSAFAs name out there and they were receiving more phone calls from people who were struggling and that was so important. To know that people were reaching out for support because I had spoken out meant so much to me, it's that memory that keeps me fighting for others and continuing to tell our story. It also keeps Chris's memory alive and is my way of honouring him. As long as people are remembered they are never truly gone.

We were even used in an online campaign by them that was being shared all over social media. J was absolutely thriving on the fact that he was giving something back, I however am not a fan of being in the limelight. That said though if it was going to help others and show people that there's help out there then I was willing to put myself out of my comfort zone. I believe that doing all of this helped to plant the seedlings of a fantastic idea that J had.

Whilst watching the Pride of Britain awards J suddenly announced to me that he'd like to raise money for SSAFA to stop other children going through what he had. I told him what a fantastic idea it was and that it was truly wonderful of him to want to help others. I explained that I was more than willing to help him, but he needed to start thinking of what he wanted to do and when he had he needed to think of what he needed to make it as good as possible. We made the deal that if he did all the planning, I would make his ideas happen to the best of my ability. I thought that would be it and that he would forget all about it, again mum was wrong!

He had a few ideas but settled with the idea of a fun day because he thought that was the best way of everyone being able to partake and enjoy themselves. So, from that point on the planning started, we contacted my contact at SSAFA, Lucy and I told her what we had planned. She was amazed and so impressed that J had come up with the idea. All the ladies in her office had fallen a little bit in love with him after the photo shoot and I think they all fell a little deeper after she told them about his idea. Lucy put me in contact with her colleague Luke who worked in the fund-raising dept. Luke and I spoke numerous times over the next few months both on the phone and over e mail, but we wouldn't actually meet until Aug '18. Although we didn't meet for so long, Luke became an important part of our life because of the support he was giving us and has become a lifetime family friend. Him and J have formed an awesome friendship and have shared lots of giggles together.

On the 2nd of August 18 we arrived at Horse Guards Parade in London for the start of the Rally for Heroes. J had been invited as a VIP and was going to start the race, although the day would be full of many surprises. We took my parents along firstly as a thank you for all they do for us and secondly because it just so happened to fall on my 40th birthday. When we arrived, we were greeted by Luke and introduced to so many people, both me and J were quite overwhelmed that all these people knew who we were. J soon composed himself though and went off with Luke to have a look at all the cars that were going to take part in the rally, their friendship was already forming at that point. Whenever I looked at J, he was having a photo taken either beside one of the very impressive cars or with some of the people taking part in the rally. It was heart-warming to see everyone wanting his attention and he handled it like a real pro. Sometimes J struggles with his confidence, not that you would know it to speak to him, but he was loving being taken to all the difference cars and having his picture taken at every opportunity.

Whilst J was off enjoying being the centre of attention, I was introduced to Sir Andrew Gregory the CEO of SSAFA. I don't think he realised quite how honoured I was that he knew who I was or that he was willing on such an important day to spend so much time with myself and J. That just shows though what a humbling and down to earth gent he really is. He explained there was going to be a service to remember all the fallen and then he would call myself and J to the podium where he would talk about all that J had done, tell our story and then give J a certificate as a thank you for raising money. This was all well and good, but we were straight after the last post which always brings a tear to my eyes even if I'm not feeling emotional so on this day it affected me more than normal. This meant that I had to stand in front of everyone with my sunglasses on but I'm sure they all understood luckily the sun was shining so I didn't look too out of place. Whilst we were stood up there J starting flossing which is a sure sign he's nervous but he had no need to be, the response he had was amazing, a huge round of applause and lots of tears were shed and not just by me. The smile on his face though when he saw how proud perfect strangers were of him was well worth all the hard work of the previous months. He got so many cuddles when the ceremony was over and so many people came over to shake my hand and tell me they were proud of me. Up until that point there had been many times when I was so immensely proud of J, but this topped them all. Sometimes you question what you are doing and if you should put yourself out there but that short amount of time with strangers proved to me that I had done the right thing and not only that but that I should keep doing it. It's hard to convey my feelings from that day, my emotions were all over the place, most of all it gave me the confidence to keep doing what we were doing and that would prove to be really important.

J was told to pick his favourite car and he could get in it and have his photo taken, well all the drivers wanted him to pick theirs, so it turned out to be more than one car he sat in! Whilst he was trying to make that difficult decision, I did an interview for BFBS TV, there was no escaping it, not even on my birthday. J then went off up the Mall and was handed a SSAFA flag that was easily bigger than him and he waved it with vigour until the last car passed through. That would have been enough to keep him smiling for weeks but no more surprises were lined up for him

We were off to the Tower of London to have a private tour by one of the Beefeaters or so I thought. There was a surprise planned for J on route that I hadn't been told about, probably for the best because I don't think I would have been able to keep my mouth shut about this one. We were taken to the Thames, so I thought maybe we were getting on one of the cruisers to the Tower. Oh no we were going on the Police boat and not only that, but J was also going to sail it down the Thames. I sat on the front of the boat waving at all the people stood on the banks, looked behind me saw J laughing with the coppers and at that point in my life I was truly truly happy. To see J having such an amazing time and to be doing something so amazing was absolutely priceless. I have to admit for fearing for my bank balance every time we went under a bridge in case, he hit the side, but I should have more faith in my wonderful son, he did a fantastic job. In fact, all the Police on the boat were trying to recruit him, I'm sure though he wouldn't take a lot of convincing. That was truly a once in a lifetime opportunity, I can't think of anyone I know that has done that, J deserved this though for always thinking of others. It was an experience neither of us will ever forget and I know J didn't want it to end.

We arrived at the Tower and were met by the rest of our party and our beefeater for the duration of the tour. What a fantastic experience that was, I'm a big fan of the Tower but to have your own personal guide who has so much knowledge of the building and its history is out of this world. J was really treated during this and was taken to see parts of the Tower others could only dream of seeing. The highlight for him was seeing where Guy Fawkes had been held because he had been learning about that at school. The highlight for mum was getting to jump the queue for the Crown Jewels and having a private talk about them before we went in.

J's amazing day was finished off with a visit to the Met Police Bomb disposal team. We started off with a talk about items they've found in the London area and all different ways people try to disguise bombs. They have such a varied display of these items from obvious devices to the much more complex. J was enthralled by the display and had so many questions, he was amazed that people were finding some of the things when digging in their gardens, in fact he wanted to dig ours up when he got home! Then came the part that J had been waiting for since we were told we were going there, we were taken outside, and he was shown inside the vans and allowed to operate the robots that they use in real life incidents. He had the EOD lads running round after him hiding objects so that he could then use the robot to find them. He was a natural at that and also a natural at hiding the objects in the most obscure places. Unfortunately for Luke on what seemed like the hottest day of the year, he ended up being chased round the courtyard by the robot. I'm not overly sure who enjoyed that most him or J. We got some amazing pictures and again it was an experience that will never be repeated or forgotten.

That brought us to the end of what can only be described as the best day of our lives so far, I couldn't have asked for a better 40th birthday and J came away with so many amazing memories, and gifts from each location, it was really a day that money couldn't buy. We've got so many photos from that day but even without them it will be fully engraved in our brains for a lifetime. All the gifts he received that day have been put in places around our home so that all our visitors can't miss them when they come round, even if they wanted to.

Although SSAFA arranged all this as a thank you for J it was so much more than that and to hear J telling people what he'd done was the point where I saw my J return. He was so full of life and smiling came easy it wasn't forced during that period and we have SSAFA to thank for that, they gave me my son back. There will never be the words to thank the people of SSAFA for what they have done and continue to do for us, their help really is lifesaving. To know that maybe we were coming out the other side was so emotional, up until that point we were still having more bad days then good, this really was the turning point in our journey.

In October 2018 I made the journey to London again but this time by myself. I was heading to the Union Jack Club near Waterloo where I hadn't been since I was on basic training many years ago. That in itself brought back so many memories of a time that seemed so long ago but what was such a huge part of my life, a period which helped to shape me into the person that I am today. SSAFA had booked me a room as I would be attending a fundraising event near Trafalgar Square and standing up to tell our story in front of a room full of strangers.

SSAFA had approached me back in the August and asked if I would be willing to do it, of course I said yes straight away. It wasn't until I sat down afterwards and really thought it through that I would be standing up in front of God knows how many people telling a story that is so personal to me and such an emotive subject. I've never been one to shy away from a challenge though and what better way to get our story out there then for me to tell it myself. I spent a while battling with myself over this, it was so important to me to help others, but it really meant putting myself completely out of my comfort zone. Let's be honest the vast majority of us don't like being somewhere where we aren't completely comfortable but sometimes it's so important that we do just that. Deep down I knew how important it was that I did this, it really was something I needed to do.

For days I sat on the sofa trying to put my thoughts onto paper, one night it flowed like a waterfall. The most difficult part was not going into too much detail, I could have talked for hours but I needed to try and concentrate on one aspect of our journey and explain just how difficult life is after suicide and how SSAFA supported us throughout the journey up to that point. I finally wrote something that I was comfortable with saying and knew that I would be confident enough to say in front of strangers. There are parts to our story that I have only started opening up about recently and that's only because I now feel able to share those parts of our lives, in a journey like this you can't force things, it has to be one day at a time.

I had so many run throughs but it's one thing to stand in your living room and bare your soul, quite different to do it in a huge room full of strangers. I videoed myself one night and showed it to numerous people that I knew would be honest with me, the response I got shocked me and I knew that I couldn't write it any better. I was on Jury service in the days leading up to the event so one day in a break I stood up in front of 30ish people and delivered my speech. This was important for me to do because I didn't know these people. I was shocked to look up whilst I was talking and see that people were in tears, to know that our story actually affects others gave me the strength to go to London and the confidence to deliver it to the best of my ability.

I'd bought a posh new dress, something I don't do very often, had my hair done, I was as ready as I was ever going to be. I had got ready a bit too early at the hotel, so I went to the bar and had a drink to calm my nerves. I felt a bit overdressed stood at a bar in an evening dress at 1700hrs but I'm sure they've seen stranger sights!! The taxi arrived and took me to the event, seeing London all lit up made me feel so at ease, it's such a beautiful place at night and it brought back memories from when I was based at RAF Northolt. I arrived at the location desperate for the loo which is a sure sign that the nerves were kicking in. I walked into the ladies and all the SSAFA girls were in there getting ready, this was the first time I had met most of them, but you would have thought I'd known them all for years. They put me at ease instantly, told me I looked beautiful, thanked me numerous times for doing this and then took me to the room where the event would take place. My first impression was WOW, not only did the room look beautiful it was absolutely huge with so many chairs set out. I had a practice run through of my speech because I've never spoken with a microphone before and the last thing, I wanted was for it to keep squeaking throughout.

I managed to get through it though whilst trying not to think about all the people that would be sitting in those chairs within the next hour. We then went through to the VIP reception where the girls had the free champagne and I made good use of the elderflower water; the way I was feeling one glass of champagne would have gone straight to my head. I was introduced to so many people in that reception and it was an honour to meet them all, but I couldn't for the life of me tell you, their names. I do however remember talking to someone very high up in the Royal Air Force and his wife, not what you'd expect from an ex-RAF Police dog handler! The whole reception went by in a blur and so quickly, that was a time in my life when I wanted it to drag, no such luck though as it so often doesn't when you really want it to.

It was time to go through and take our seats, after the starter it was my turn to stand up, Sir Andrew Gregory was doing an introduction for me, it doesn't get much more important than that. I managed to walk to and on the stage without tripping which for me in heals is an achievement in itself. I reached the podium, took a deep breath and took my first step into public speaking. Although I was looking around during the speech, I didn't really take anyone in I was so focused on delivering the speech the best way I keep and also trying to keep my emotions in check. At one point I looked up and saw a lady smiling at me, so I tried to use her as a focus point. If she's reading this then I would like to take this opportunity to say thank you because you really helped me get through that speech.

The first thing I noticed when I finished was the sound of applause, when I looked up every single person was up on their feet, some were wiping their eyes, and some were smiling at me, but I had touched every single person in there and I couldn't be prouder of myself. It was an odd feeling that our story had touched so many people, it's emotional for us but I never quite realised the effect it would have on others. Walking back to my seat people were trying to talk to me but I had my head down and I needed to get back to the girls. All the emotions I had been holding in were getting dangerously close to the surface, in fact a few tears had already escaped. It was a strange emotion, I wasn't upset but I was completely overwhelmed, a feeling I'm not used to. Imagine my surprise upon sitting down when the then Secretary of State for Defence Gavin Williamson came over to congratulate me and ask me how he was supposed to follow that! Every time I moved around the room it took me twice as long to get anywhere because people wanted to talk to me. It was such an amazing feeling to know that that these people were not only listening to me but also that they would take something away from this. Being listened to meant that Chris's death wasn't in vain, and I had high hopes that from here on in maybe changes would be made. It was a truly amazing night, and I was thankful for the response I got, definitely another night I won't forget.

On the 10th of November Mum and I travelled to London to the Royal Albert Hall for the Festival of Remembrance, we were in the SSAFA box with two other veterans, their partners and Sir Andrew Gregory and his wife. This is something I've always wanted to go to and when we arrived and saw our seats it was a dream come true. We were sitting right next to the top of the steps where people marched down, and we were just round from the Royal Box. Now I don't know about you but when I watch this on the TV I spend the whole time in tears, actually being there was 100% more emotional. Being so close to all the people taking part was humbling and with it being the 100-year anniversary the whole festival was so much more emotional. J was watching it at home with Grandad seeing if he could spot us which he did numerous times. I made the mistake of going to the loo during the performance. It was a mistake because the box doors don't have a handle on the outside and I couldn't get back in. I was very conscious that if I knocked too loudly I might disturb something to do with the festival. One of the serving soldiers however had no such fear and knocked so loud it would have woken the dead. It was great to talk to the other Veterans in the box and discuss the different ways that SSAFA had helped all three of us. I remember looking at the Royal Marine Veteran next to me during the service and seeing a tear roll down his cheek, it didn't shock me though and I knew he was having some of the same thoughts as me in that moment. We didn't get home till gone midnight so it was a long day but it's definitely something that will stay with me forever and I have SSAFA to thank for giving me the chance to be there. I'm so glad I got the chance to share that with my mum, she's my best friend and my rock and it felt good to be able to give her the chance to experience that.

In 2021 yet again I travelled to London again but this time I was going to be even further out of my comfort zone, I was filming a TV advert! I'm sure if you could track down my Drama teacher from high school, they would agree that acting is not one of my skills. However, this was for a charity I believe in, and it was about our story, therefore how I portrayed myself in it was how it should be, I'm not sure the director agreed though. As soon as I got there, I had my hair and make up done and this was constantly touched up during the day, not my idea of fun. We did have one stumbling block, we were filming in a cold warehouse, and I had the problem that many women will understand so I had to borrow a cardigan and wear it in a certain way. It turned out to be a very long day, both mentally and physically exhausting but I knew something special had been achieved. That was proved to me when I saw the final edit, it was both hard hitting and emotional, I knew it would have the desired effect.

I received so many messages when it started being aired and not a single bad point in all of them which in itself is an achievement. It's something that I will be extremely proud of for years to come.

I've spoken a lot during this chapter about the help that SSAFA have given me what I haven't done is thank them. There are so many people behind the scenes that have been there for us both during this period but there are a few that stand out, hopefully they know who they are. Both myself and J thank these from the bottom of our hearts. I thank SSAFA as a whole though for helping J to smile again and for giving me the opportunity to tell my story and for giving me the courage to do that. Without SSAFA neither of us would be where we are now, the help they have given us has been truly lifesaving.

Charity Fun Day

After having the idea of a fun day J started making lists (definitely gets his love of lists from me) of what he wanted there, this started off quite small bouncy castle, raffle, tombola and maybe an inflatable assault course. This was all completely doable and would be great as a local fun day. His first target was to raise £200 but he did say even if he only raised £5 that could be enough to help someone and that was his main aim from all of this to help others. He wasn't doing this to be on the TV and radio, he was doing this because he had lost his daddy through the worst possible circumstances and didn't want it to happen to others. That was his only motivation, and it was all his own choice and at no point was he influenced by anything other than his own passion. I started ringing round inflatable companies to see if we could get any good deals, the best company I found was Dave's Inflatables in Suffolk, we spoke about the different deals they could sort for us but obviously we needed a date and a location. Well little man came up with probably the best location ever, his school. What a prime location, it's the heart of the village, it's signposted, and it has a huge field. The next step was to get a meeting with the head teacher Mrs Murray which happened within days, J made that a bit easier as when I walked in, he had already spoken to her about it! You can always rely on J to pave the way for you, that boy couldn't keep a secret if his life depended on it, just like any other 9-year-old. We decided on a date 2nd June 2018 and then it was all systems go. I went home and booked a bouncy castle, inflatable slide and water stocks, which seemed to be the most important parts in J's mind. Whilst J was designing posters to ask people for donations I started writing to local and national companies asking for raffle prizes, I must have sent out 100 letters and I wasn't overly confident about replies but the more you send the higher the chances of a positive response are.

I made a Facebook group and invited everyone I knew; this was the best way I could think of to get it out there what J had planned. From that the event started to grow, people asked if they could have stalls there to sell crafts etc, I made the decision to say yes and decided to charge a fee of £10, although on the day a lot of people paid more as there were so many people there. It was another way to raise more money and all the stall holders have their own followers so it would advertise the event even further. Every little was going to help in both the fund raising and getting people to attend. I was still fixed on the idea that it would be a small local fun day though.

I collared one of my friends in the playground one morning, Liz, she was part of the PTA and extremely good and experienced at organising events. As soon as I mentioned what J was planning then she was more than happy to help us, a decision she may have regretted. Cue the start of lots of meetings between us when I had a day off, lots of lists and lots of half-drunk brews. After seeing the response, we were getting on the Facebook page we thought maybe we could make this a little bit bigger than what was originally planned. We made a long list of things we could have there and then I went through it with J, and he chose the things he wanted. This included a military band, circus performer, military cars amongst others. As you can tell from that small list his plans had grown hugely with time, this was going to be bigger than we first thought, a lot bigger. He was getting so excited about it and everyday thought of different things he could have there.

We were approached on the page about maybe speaking to the local Army Cadets in Framlingham to see if they were interested in attending. I spoke to the lady in charge, Michelle and she was more than happy for them to attend and to do a drill demo. Well, that took this to a whole new level and meant we would need an arena, which also meant we'd need other people to fill it. We spoke to Chloe Kinrade who runs a local dance class that J actually used to attend, she was thrilled to be asked to attend and couldn't wait to tell her classes about it. This was exciting because it would also bring in all the relatives of the dancers and I knew that Chloe taught a lot of youngsters. We said to Chloe that the dancers wouldn't need to pay to come in, but their relatives would, I knew once in the dancers would use their charms on theirs parents to spend money!

I started to phone around to try and source a Military Band but after speaking to a few different contacts it seemed they would cost in the region of £300 which was something we just didn't have. This was about raising money not dipping into the profits before we had even started. After a comment on the events page, I got in touch with the RAF Honington Band who were happy to attend for free. Fantastic, there's nothing quite like a real forces band to get people in the mood for enjoying themselves. Also, this was another fantastic show that could go in the arena, the band was happy to go in twice, so they were booked to open and close the event, what better way to start and end an event for a Forces charity. I was so excited about the band as I love hearing proper military music and they had a treat in store for J on the day when he was able to be the conductor for a song, luckily, they knew what they were doing because I don't think anyone could have followed his exaggerated waving of the baton. That was another awesome experience though and one that he thoroughly enjoyed.

I put the posters that J had made up at work asking for donation prizes and we started to be inundated with various gifts all of which made fantastic prizes. J also decided that he wanted to do a sweet tombola and a teddy on a string tombola. As you can tell this event was getting bigger by the day which meant we were going to have to advertise far and wide to get the people through the gates. It's all very good to have lots of stands and attractions at an event but no good if you can't get people through the gate, I think this was my biggest concern. It was like when you organise a birthday party and worry that no one will attend but on a much bigger scale, it was the cause of many sleepless nights.

Liz was working hard in the background and secured an article in our local newspaper and an interview on Radio Suffolk. This was the same radio station that I had spoken to in the lead up to Armistice Day, so they already knew our story. J made such a good impression on the radio he was completely at ease doing it, it was nice to see him so comfortable yet also so excited about what he was planning. My fear was it was live and you're never quite sure what will come out of kids mouths. That fear was realised when Mark Murphy asked J what he thought of Norwich City FC and J said, 'they suck'. The comment however meant we got some wonderful donations from Ipswich Town FC who apparently loved his comment. Mark Murphy, his team and his listeners have all been a great source of support to us both throughout everything we have done and have been so generous. This gave us a huge amount of free advertising because of the reach of the radio station. We also secured a TV interview with ITV Anglia news which J loved doing and he also got some of his friends involved in that. That was great because it gave it a real community feel which J wanted, he wanted the community to come together, and he certainly achieved that. Liz was also busily trying to secure some sponsorship for the event, there have to be some outgoings, but we didn't want those costs to come out of the profits. Some wonderful local businesses came forward which meant we could book everything that J wanted on the day so a huge thank you to all of those companies. Radio Suffolk started a campaign to find teddies and sweets for the event which was a huge success, and we owe a huge thank you to Mark Murphy's breakfast crew. J was amazed when one of the reporters from the station arrived at ours one day with numerous teddies, sweets and other donations.

I could talk for pages about the preparation that went into the day and all the people that helped make it what it was but all I really need to say is that not just the local community came together but the whole county and even people from further afield. There are so many people that we need to thank for their donations and assistance on the day, but I'm scared of missing someone out so a huge thank you to you all and without you the day couldn't have happened, and it certainly wouldn't have been the success that it was. You all helped a 10-year-old to achieve something beyond his wildest dreams and more importantly than that you proved to him that you care.

I do however need to single a few people out; mum and dad were amazing as always, they spent hours attaching posters to boards and putting them all around the county. They paid for the insurance for the day which without that the event couldn't go on. They secured donations, prizes, sold raffle tickets, organised volunteers for the day and helped out themselves. More importantly they helped keep me sane in the months leading up to the day which was paramount to me keeping going. Liz Quickenden gave up so much of her spare time to help me and J organise things. Also, though it all she was support for me, I hadn't realised just how emotional organising this would be, but all the interviews brought everything back and so many tears were shed, Liz was always there with a hug and a brew at the exact right moment. Finally, Woody from Rainywood photography offered his services for the day and also gave us the rights to all the pictures taken, that in itself was worth hundreds and appreciated more then he'll ever know. Woody has been involved in another fundraiser with us since and again took some wonderful photographs.

The day of the event arrived, and I was awake from 4am, between nerves and worrying about the weather sleep eluded me that night. I checked the weather on my phone repeatedly and it just kept getting worse, thunderstorms were predicted for the 4hrs the event was planned. I was keeping the faith though they had been predicting these storms for at least 3 weeks although I was still petrified. When J got up at half six, he told me not to worry and that his dad would make sure the weather was fine. Quite an in depth thought from a 10-year-old I thought, and I had to follow his lead, he'd already proved me wrong on numerous occasions.

We arrived at the school and met with numerous others to get everything set up. This was probably the most stressed I'd been since J came up with the idea, mainly due to the nagging feeling that people wouldn't attend the event. At half eleven most things were ready to go, the outside stalls had arrived, inflatables were blown up and the bar b q was lit. At 12 the gates opened and for the first time in my life I was lost for words, the queues to get in were bigger than I could ever imagine and just to add to my amazement the sun came out. J was right his dad was certainly looking out for him that day. Right up until 3 o'clock there were queues at the gates to get in, I'd been worrying we'd have too many prizes on the tombola's I was now worrying we wouldn't have enough. We had completely over ordered at Swiss farm for the bar b q food (who gave us a fantastic deal) and we ran out at 3 o'clock, I had been putting off getting a burger thinking there would be plenty, so I made do with an ice cream. Every single stall had crowds round them and the arena was 3 people deep around all 4 sides. I dread to think how many steps I did that day, but I know I didn't stop for hours just like many others. Although at one point I went and locked myself in my car for 5 minutes just to give myself a breather and time to reflect. It would have been extremely emotional if I had allowed myself to think about it. My 10-year-old son had achieved this, it was his interviews that had encouraged people to come, it was his wonderful personality that had charmed so many. It just shows what can be achieved if you want it enough and if you are willing to put yourself out there. To do what he did at such a young age shows exactly what sort of person he is.

The way the community pulled together for a 10-year-old who was going through something a lot of adults don't cope with was inspirational and I know that J was blown away. I didn't see a lot of him that day because everyone wanted a bit of him, there were 2 TV crews there and everyone wanted to talk to him. I did see him every now and then either doing somersaults on the bouncy castle or running about with his mates Jack and Miles. The way he coped with all the attention that day made me the proudest mum in the world, he showed everyone what I already knew, that he's a well-balanced, good mannered, cheeky young man. When he made a speech before we did the raffle, I don't think there was a dry eye in the crowd. When J talks about his dad then he speaks right from the heart, he's so open about it which makes it so powerful, I think people are sometimes shocked by how honest he is, and it makes you catch your breath. He speaks way beyond his years and really makes you stop and listen. J has so many wonderful memories from that day, he did drill with the cadets and made such an impression on them they asked him to march with them as a VIP on Remembrance Day. The ice cream vendor gave him free ice creams all day, which of course went down very well with him. There are many more memories but the one thing that struck me was every time I saw him, he was smiling or laughing, he really was in his element. Although he did this to help others it was also huge in helping him with the healing process.

We eventually got home at 6pm that night, both of us were completely exhausted, mentally and physically. After ordering a takeaway we set about the enormous task of counting the money, we didn't have a clue where to start, there seemed to be so much, not just coins but so many notes as well. I face timed Liz after getting all the money together in one big pile and when she saw the size of the task ahead of us, she drove over to help. The funniest part was when I announced to J that we had over £1000 in twenty-pound notes. Bearing in mind his target was £200 he was just blown away. As it turns out he raised just under £6000, an absolutely amazing achievement and he was understandably extremely proud of himself, me, I was speechless. I couldn't quite believe just how generous people had been and that total was only going to grow.

Radio Suffolk phoned us on the Monday morning to find out how the event went which gave us the opportunity to thank all those that had supported J. Mark Murphy was very nearly shocked into silence when J announced how much he had raised. The East Anglian Daily Times also ran a piece in the days after the event and we thank them as well for their support. The reach they both gave us before the event was amazing and through them both so many donations were made. From this article a lot of people made contact wanting to make donations, one of them a large amount and it took the money raised to just under £7000.

We split the money equally between the Suffolk branch of SSAFA and the main branch in London. We did this because it was the Suffolk branch i.e., Sue that had helped us when Chris first died, and we wanted to be able to give back to them. It's important to J to be able to help as many veterans as possible which is why we donated the rest of the money to the London branch so that it could be used country wide. The whole of SSAFA were amazed by the amount raised and so very grateful to J. I don't think Luke quite knew what to say when I emailed him to let him know how it went, I do know that he couldn't say thank you enough. Thanks weren't needed though; this was our way of thanking them and helping others.

Over the next few weeks life slowed down a considerable amount and gave me a chance to think. Here was a young man that at the age of 8 was given some of the worst news possible and he then had to try and process it whilst dealing with the unnatural feeling of grief. Not only did he want to say thank you to the wonderful charity that had helped us he also wanted to stop this happening to others. I am humbled that J is my son and inspired by the way he has dealt with everything he has been through. When I look at him, I know I've done something right in my life. He is the one person that can make me smile when I want to cry, he makes me laugh with hardly any effort, he also knows how to press every single one of my buttons. I wouldn't change him for anything though, I love the way he has found his own personality and just enjoys being him.

As I reach the end of this chapter let me say again how much we appreciate every single person that helped in every single way to make this wonderful event happen.

Awards and Appearances

J came home from school one day with a letter addressed to parent of Jamie Small, I had no idea what this was about and was actually quite impressed that J hadn't opened it, that was probably a first and something most parents can sympathise with. Upon reading it my eyes welled up, J had been short listed for the most inspirational under 12-year-old in Suffolk in the Raising the Bar awards. This is something that is organised by Suffolk County Council and held in Trinity Park in Ipswich. I told J that he had been short listed and explained that hundreds of people will have been nominated and that if he didn't win to come in the top 3 was a huge achievement. Of course, I thought that J should win but I'm biased, and I knew that there would be some tough competition as there's so many wonderful kids out there.

The night of the awards arrived, and we got ourselves dressed up, J was thrilled to be in a suit and tie which was good because it was something he would be wearing lots in the future. We met J's head teacher Mrs Murray and his favourite teacher Mr Woods there and soon it was time for the evening to start so we took our seats. J was called up with 2 other extremely inspirational young men and all 3 nominations were read out, then came the moment, the winner was read out. I had prepared myself that J wouldn't win and after hearing all the stories all 3 boys were worthy of the award. I was to be proved wrong and they announced J as the winner, just when you think you can't be prouder of your son then he pulls that out of the bag. I may have had a bit of grit in my eyes when J sat down and he asked me why I was crying, that's something he'll understand when he's a parent. Another mum sat at the table explained to him that mums are strange creatures and that when we are happy or proud, we tend to cry, he shrugged his shoulders and dug into the food in front of him. Mrs Murray and Mr Woods were just as proud as me and as soon as there was a break in proceedings, I phoned my parents to let them now, they were both over the moon as you can imagine and extremely proud.

J spent the rest of the evening sitting there with a huge smile on his face looking at his trophy, proud as punch. I don't think I'd ever been as proud of J as I was in that moment, although there were a lot more moments ahead where I would feel that again, I knew he was a special young man but to know that had been recognised but people around him was the most amazing feeling. Again, he had to have his picture taken copious amounts, but he was becoming an old pro at that, he seems to be at his happiest in front of a camera and knows exactly what pose to pull. So many people congratulated him and told him he should be so proud of himself. I think looking back it all passed in a bit of a blur for J, but he definitely enjoyed it although I think he'd admit to being a bit surprised. It was a wonderful evening and so many amazing people were celebrated. It was definitely a night that neither of us will ever forget and a massive achievement that can never be taken away from him.

The next amazing thing to happen was an e mail from Ipswich Town football Club, they asked J to be a Community Champion at the game of his choice. There was only one game in his mind and that was the local derby against Norwich City Football Club, it must be all young football fans dream to lead their team out against their biggest rivals, I know it was always mine. Before the day J received a letter from Luke Chambers the Ipswich captain saying how proud the whole team was to meet J and to congratulate him on his achievements. That's been safely put away in a scrap book with other important memories of his journey – it's quite full! Although J will always be a Liverpool fan Ipswich are his local team and he always enjoys going to watch them play.

We arrived at Portman Road on the morning of the match along with my parents and my brother Adrian. Myself, dad, and my brother are all huge Ipswich fans, my mum has been known to attend quite a few games over the years. As the person though who fell asleep during the game in which we were crowned champions of the league whilst a Mexican wave was going on, I think she'll admit to not being footballs greatest fan. We were all full of excitement that is always around on derby day, J was kitted out in his new Ipswich strip that he was proud as punch to be wearing, I was more worried that he was rapidly out growing it when it had cost a small fortune. When we arrived, we were shown to one of the VIP areas where we were given a team sheet and a programme, we all had something to eat and a drink. J was starting to go a bit quiet at this point, so I knew the nerves were starting to kick in, hardly surprising considering it was a maximum crowd and being shown on the TV. My parents and brother were shown to their seats whilst myself and J were escorted onto the side of the pitch where we were watching the teams warm up. J actually looked giddy when the Ipswich players were running past him, it was amazing to watch him up close with some of his heroes. I was pretty much the same though and a bit star struck as the players wandered passed us with a few high fives for J, mum was rightly ignored during this. Not that I would have been able to string a proper sentence together anyway.

We were both interviewed at the side of the pitch which was pretty mind blowing and the response we got from the crowd was out of this world. J then got to present Gwion Edwards with the player of the month trophy and a bottle of champagne just before all the players went back to the changing rooms. I must admit I was also in my element having been an Ipswich fan since I was 4 years old, being this close to the players was a bit of a dream for me. We waited in the tunnel whilst we were waiting for the players to come out and who should come out and talk to J but Paul Hurst the manager at the time. They had a quick chat and then J taught him how to floss, quite a claim to fame! It was lovely that he came out to speak to J though and really proved that Ipswich Town is a family club through and through.

It was then time for the players to come out, so I moved back out to the side of the pitch ready to take numerous photos and J waited with the community officer. Then came his moment of fame, J walked out with the referee and the linesman, picked the match ball up off a podium and led both teams out to the centre circle. He then stood with the ref and shook hands or got a pat on the shoulder of every player on both teams. He then got to have photos taken with the mascots and Luke Chambers before running off the pitch to rousing applause from the crowd. We made our way to our seats when the mascot walked in front of where we were sat so J ran off to get a cuddle and a high five from him.

Unfortunately, the curse that has followed Ipswich for years in regard to the derby game showed its ugly face again that day and after being the better team for most of the match it finished 1-1. That however couldn't dampen J's mood and he was flying high for weeks afterwards. He especially loved it when he went football training on the Monday afterwards and a lot of his team had been at the game, so they had all seen him. That definitely gave him bragging rights for weeks and his teammates had so many questions and were full of praise for him.

To get selected to do something like that is a once in a lifetime chance and something that again J will never forget. Childhood is all about making good memories and this was definitely something that J can tell his kids and grandchildren about in years to come. One thing you can easily say about ITFC is that it's a family club and the wonderful way we were treated by them for that whole time is something that will stay with us for years. I hope if they read this, they realise what a difference they made to a young man's life so thank you.

The community came together again for J when the nominations for Pride of Britain opened, well not just the community but people country wide, I dread to think how many nominations he got! It wasn't to be though and although J didn't win it was a huge achievement to have got so many nominations. J knew that he had been nominated and obviously also knew that he hadn't won but he happily sat down to watch the awards and said how much the young man who won deserved it. I loved the way he was so mature over it whereas a lot of people would believe they deserved to win. Not J though he was just happy that the judges had heard about what he had done and would have seen what work SSAFA do.

Grief

The most important thing I can say in this book is that grief affects every single person differently and we all deal with it in completely different ways. There's no manual to tell you how to cope or what to do, you have to do what's right for you at the time. What works for one person will not necessarily work for another and vice versa, it's so important that you give yourself time and find your own way.

To start with I wasn't sure what I was supposed to feel, we were separated after all, should I be grieving, and more importantly did I have the right to grieve? The answer to that was yes, I had loved him for over 10 years, and he was the father of our son I had every right to cry over him. I think the reason I struggled with that was I was receiving messages that would start, 'I know you weren't together'. Why should that make a difference, I was the one who supported him through tours, kept the family together until it became dangerous. I had every right to cry over him, but I cried over the man I'd fallen in love with not the man that had died.

When we first heard about Chris, I thought I needed to be strong for J and by doing that I thought I shouldn't cry in front of him. I was wrong, he needed to see me cry and needed to see that there was nothing wrong in that. It took me weeks to figure that out but once I did it seemed like a weight had been lifted off my shoulders. Yes, I was still crying myself to sleep but I wasn't trying to stifle my tears and they weren't quite so bad because I would have already shed a few tears with J whilst talking about Chris and having cuddles on the sofa. Night times were definitely the worst times though, when you can't sleep, and you are just left alone with your thoughts. Grief would hit in waves then and there was nothing I could do except cry it out.

After I accepted all this J began to open up a bit more, part of our grief was to talk about him and look at photos. To start with this didn't help us smile and it would always end in tears with J asking questions about why it had happened. Those are questions that I wasn't willing to answer at the time, but I have told J I'll explain everything when he's older. He knew that daddy died because he wasn't well and that he struggled hugely with life after things he'd seen whilst in the Army. I'm not sure when I'll think he's old enough to know all of the facts but I'm sure when he's ready it'll click into place, and I'll know that it's the right time to sit him down and explain everything. I'm also sure that J will let me know when he's ready as well and on things like this I have to follow his lead.

I made an album of photos, mainly for J but for my benefit as well. When I was going through all the albums on the laptop choosing pictures it brought back so many memories, memories I had locked away but memories I was glad to relive. All of these were of happier times, and it cut me to the deep that we would be making no more of those and if I didn't remember them, they would be forgotten forever. Some of the photos had J in them from when he was tiny so of course he couldn't remember those times so it was up to me to tell the stories so that Chris can live on through them, if I don't tell them, they will be forgotten forever. After a few months we were able to look through the pictures and not just smile but laugh when we remembered things and that was a huge part of us being able to move on.

At school with one of the teachers J decorated a box that he could use as a memory box. That turned out to be a wonderful idea and helped J a lot to know that he could look through it and everything in there would bring back a different memory. There are so many things in there, Chris's watch, his full-size medals, photos, driving licence, wallet, his pass to Euro Disney and his beret amongst other things. It's on top of his wardrobe now and he doesn't get it out very often, but he knows it's there and that he can look in it any time he wants. I think sometimes it helps to know that a part of his dad is nearby, he doesn't have to look at it all the time because he knows it's there and that helps him more than looking in it every day.

Something J wanted to do when we decorated his room in our old flat was to put pictures of his dad on his wall which we did and there were also pictures scattered around in there as well. In our new home he hasn't put pictures on the wall because he said it upset him sometimes, knowing that he would never see his dad again. This was completely J's choice and I respect his decision and how he wants to deal with things. We have however got his miniature medals in the wall unit in the living room, and we have got some of his ashes in a memory stone in there as well. For a while when J went to bed, he would kiss the photos goodnight which used to break my heart when I went in his room and saw the lip marks on the photos. He used to speak to them, that could have been him saying he misses him, or he loves him, or it could entail him getting angry. Since he put the pictures away, he seems to be processing it all better, again he knows where the pictures are, and he can get them out whenever he wants. This of course may change in the future, and he may want them back up on the wall again, that's fine, whatever works for and helps him.

Part of the grief process is anger and we've both been through that, with me it was quite early on, and I showed it in so many different ways. Sometimes I would get angrier and angrier seeing things posted online by people that hadn't been there for Chris but were making out they couldn't be closer. Sometimes I would talk to Chris, but it was definitely not the sort of chat that would have put a smile on his face. It helped me though to get my feelings out and to vent at him although I know that I'll never get the answers that I need to completely make my peace with it. That's the hardest part, we will never fully get closure because there's so many questions, we will never get an answer to. J has been angry, so angry that those that know him wouldn't believe it was the same boy, it's so hard to watch your son being eaten up by such a negative feeling, especially when you know that nothing you do will make it better for him, I can't bring his dad back and that's what he truly wants. What I can do though is cuddle him, tell him I love him and tell him that what he's feeling is normal and eventually it will get easier, or if not easier then you learn to cope with it. Because of that I let him do what he needed to do, if he wanted to hit or kick something he used a cushion, if he wanted to shout, he shouted and there's been a few swear words as well, although he always asks permission before that one. I think it's been good for him however hard it's been for me to watch, there are so many thoughts going through his head and at such a young age it's so hard for him to know how to process them. He did have counselling, but he didn't really bond with the counsellor, which is so important, so he ended up not really engaging with her. We haven't given up on that though and as soon as J says he wants to give it another go I will find someone for him.

I talk to Chris normally as well and I can just imagine what his answers would be and it's like I'm having a proper conversation with him. Although that's not something I do as much now, that doesn't mean I've forgotten him, or I don't think of him because that couldn't be further from the truth. I've never been a huge believer of the afterlife but at times I've been 110% certain that Chris has been with me and it's like I can feel him behind me with his hands on my shoulders like he used to when I was upset. I still dream about him to this day and on a few occasions, I would swear blind I've seen him but when I look back there's no one there. I've caught J staring at nothing before now and then he'll give his head a shake and a smile will appear, and I know what he's seen. I have to believe now though that there is something when we die because I can't cope with the thought that Chris just ceased to exist. The way I see it is that he will continue to exist as long as he is remembered and spoken about.

J has coped so well with his grief, better than some adults have in fact, to start with he had so many more bad days then good, and I really struggled to see his heart breaking. The one thing he did struggle with was his feelings and understanding why he felt the way he did. The aftermath of that is J often looks on the negatives of himself, he focuses on things that have been bad or he finds negatives about himself. I've worked so hard on trying to teach him to look for the positives, we now write down a positive from every day and put it in a pot, that seems to be working. He's always tried to remember the good things about his dad which I encourage but in the same breath I don't want him to hero worship. This is all part of the grieving process we don't want to think bad of someone that's no longer here, I was certainly guilty of this when Chris first died. In time though we've managed to remember both the good and bad things about him, remembering the bad doesn't mean we don't love him it just means we remember the real Chris, after all no one is perfect. It is much easier to find peace with your grief when you remember the full story, Chris was Chris, warts and all and that's how we will remember him.

There is no right or wrong way to grieve for someone you have to do what feels right for you and whatever gets you through it. I've searched my soul so many times questioning if I could have changed what happened, but my conscience is clear. The last time I saw Chris, I told him that I would be there for him whatever, no matter what had happened between us. He chose to reach out to someone else though, someone that was supposed to love him, and she turned her back on him. I struggle with that hugely because we will never know if it had been dealt with differently what the outcome would have been. A lot of my anger has been directed towards that person which has worked for me, I've never met her and I'm never likely to but it's just the way I feel and I'm not going to question that. Although over time that anger has lessened and if anything, I feel more pity for them. After all they are the ones that have to live with their themselves.

As I've mentioned earlier when Chris first died, I got so many messages on social media, an awful lot from people whom I wasn't friends with and I'm sure Chris hadn't spoken to them in a while. Some of the messages were lovely, sending their condolences and their love to me and J, some were just fishing for information. I tried to reply to them all at least with a thank you, I gave out no further information to them because it was up to me what people knew. It was already common knowledge that Chris had taken his own life I didn't really understand why people needed to know more than that. A lot of posts appeared all over a certain social media page about what a good mate Chris had been and what a fab person he was, where were all these people when Chris needed them though? It's like they had to clear any guilt they felt by making out how close they were, I knew from what Chris had said to me in the Feb before he died that most of those had washed their hands of him, those are his words. There were friends though that did their best for him, and I know of one that feels extremely guilty, but I wish he wouldn't. Chris wouldn't want him to live with that burden and I don't want him too either. I beg of you though when you are messaging or speaking to someone that is grieving, please think about what you are saying, a few wrong words can cut so deep, and it can take a long time to recover from that.

The thing to remember is that grief comes in waves, for a week you can be thinking 'wow I've got this' then all of a sudden you hear a certain song and you're sat there in floods of tears. Chris has been gone for over 5 years when I write this, and it still hurts just as much as the day he died, and I still find myself welling up when I tell people about it but not as much as I used to. I don't think the pain will ever go completely and it doesn't necessarily get easier with time like people say but I think you do learn to cope with it and to live with it. This is now our new normal, life will never be what it once was, but we do have a life and it's a good one.

Now we have so many more good days then bad and when we talk about Chris, we do it with a smile on our faces and lots of laughter. We still think about him often and he's never far from our thoughts, but we are learning that life goes on. I know that Chris would want us to live our lives to the full and that's what we're trying to do in his memory.

Life Goes On

The best piece of advice I've been given throughout all of this is that it was Chris that died not us. This may sound harsh to some, but it most certainly wasn't meant in a bad way but to reassure us that it's fine for us to live our lives and not to feel guilty for that. Life does go on though and however hard that is we can't live in the past because that would just destroy us. As I mentioned previously, I've forgiven Chris for everything that happened between us and how he was afterwards, I had to do that to be able to move on otherwise it would have crippled me inside and left me extremely bitter, that's just not me. Some of the things he put me through were so painful but not as painful as his untimely death, maybe that has put things in perspective for me. His death has taught me a lot though and it's given me so much more strength than I thought possible and also shown me that I am stronger than I thought. I have cut the negatives out of our lives and learnt to surround ourselves with positives, people don't get as many chances these days, if you upset either of us then you are gone, especially if you upset J. I have no hesitation in cutting you out of our lives if you don't have our best interests at heart or you try and hurt us in any way. It would be so very easy to live in the past and to dwell on why we were dealt the hand that we were but instead we are learning to turn that into a positive. We have been given a voice and we need to use that to help others. By doing what we do we keep Chris alive, but I know he would want us to live a full and exciting life.

J's life is moving on far too rapidly for me, he's now in his third year of high school and is about to start working towards his GCSE's, it only seems like 5 minutes ago he was starting school in Germany. He settled in well and is working as hard as he did in primary school, the number of subjects was a bit of a shock though and it sometimes takes extra persuasion where homework is concerned. To me he looks far too small to be going there but I'm proud of how he has embraced it just like he does everything else, and he'll thrive under the challenge of the hard work. He has a fantastic attitude towards schoolwork and understands that he needs to work hard to make his dreams come true. I know that he'll achieve whatever he sets his mind to because failure just isn't in his mindset. Covid has meant that he hasn't had the experience of High School that he was expecting although he got to go to lockdown school as I was a keyworker. He loved that and it enabled the teachers to really get to know him as there were so few students in.

Unfortunately, J has had to overcome so many hurdles in his life and one of the biggest is being on the receiving end of bullying. It turns out that the child who was doing this was jealous of the attention that J has received over the last few years. I find it extremely sad that upon hearing about and seeing the child's behaviour that the parent didn't sit them down and explain that J would much rather have his dad here then the attention. Although it's sometimes hard to work out who is the most jealous, the parent or the child. Although to be bullied is awful it made J stronger, to be able to walk away from someone that is hitting out at you or saying extremely cruel things will always make J the stronger person. It makes me proud that through all of this he still cares about others and not just as a person but how they are feeling. He hates to see anyone upset and it really affects him when people are angry, I do believe though that some of that stems from memories of his dad returning from Afghan. Although this happened in Primary school it was something certain kids did in High School as well, it started off as verbal bullying but ended up with six young adults attacking him outside of school. I reached my limit when this happened and involved the local Police who were fantastic from start to finish and it was dealt with quickly. The people involved did make the mistake of coming to our door trying to lure J out, there may not be a man here, but they didn't bank on me either and they haven't been back since. The school were extremely supportive as well and put lots of things in place for J which really helped him. They recently had a workshop on bullying, and he stood up in front of his peers and said that he wanted all the comments and bullying to stop which reduced some to tears. He has received a lot of apologies since which he accepted but doesn't trust but now, he is like a different boy. From this bullying grew the idea of another Fun Day which he is busy planning as I write this. However, this time he is raising money for Scotty's Little Soldiers, SSAFA and Hidden Warriors CIC, all of which have supported him.

J's main love in life is sports, he can turn his hand to the majority of them with a bit of hard work. He has represented his primary school in various team sports ranging from netball to touch rugby. He played for a local football team, Benhall Badgers Cubs who are a fantastic bunch of kids and they make a fantastic team. Whilst playing for them he came on leaps and bounds both in his confidence and his skill. A lot of that is down to hard work on his part but credit also has to be paid to his coach Dean Barker. Dean has been a good friend of mine for more years than I care to remember and happens to be married to my best friend Gail. The support that Dean has given to J since we moved back to Suffolk has been second to none and J looks up to him as a father figure. All the lads in that team are so lucky to have a coach that cares about their success so much.

J loved doing gymnastics which he did for three years. He luckily got a place at Pipers Vale in Ipswich soon after we moved back, they had a fantastic set up and J absolutely loved going there. He worked through his grades quite quickly only having to redo his grade 2 but soon found himself in the advanced rec class. There is a huge jump between the two classes, but he slowly made his way through the awards although he had a love hate relationship with the pommel horse. He had a great friendship with his previous coach Adam Steele who just so happens to be an Irish international gymnast, a fact that J is extremely proud of. He was then coached by Cameron who is a Scottish International and like Adam has helped Jamie considerably. His biggest hero in the world of gymnastics is Nile Wilson and J has said on more than one occasion that he is his inspiration. I once tweeted Nile Wilson and he re-tweeted and replied which absolutely made Jamie's year, I think he told everyone he knew!

J started playing table tennis with my dad and has already represented his High School in a competition. He attended a club in Ipswich which he really enjoyed, and it was great to see him improve every single week. Unfortunately, due to the corona virus all training stopped so practiced on the dining room table! It's also something he can play with my parents, brother and myself as we all play although he's starting to get far too good for me and I have no chance of returning his smash! He chose not to continue with this after lockdown although he still plays at school, instead he decided to give Karate a go. Well, he has certainly found his niche in life with that, and he has truly excelled and is flying through the belts. He did his first competition in January 22 and placed 3rd in the sparring which was amazing. A huge thank you to Hidden Warriors CIC for helping with his Karate you have certainly put a smile on his face.

I've spoken of how different ways of coping work for different people, I went back to work quite early on after losing Chris, this maybe wouldn't work for everyone, but it worked for me. I needed and I believe J needed routine and normality to our lives and I would do exactly the same again. Work were so fantastic during that extremely hard period, it would be so hard to single out certain people, but I believe some do need a special thank you. Whilst I worked on the ward Bec's, Angela and Debs were my rocks, they could take one look at my face and know exactly what I was feeling or if I needed 5 minutes just for me. Bec's especially has been a wonderful role model and friend to Jamie, although I'm not sure which has the highest mental age! Jo, who was the housekeeper, has become a friend for life and although she now works in a different dept it won't stop the get togethers. When I moved across into a therapy role, I already knew of the staff obviously, but I didn't really know them or them me. Again, there are some truly wonderful people who work in that department but all the rehab girls, Hetty, Gill, Sue, Roisin, Moira and Lou are the ones who always remembered certain dates and asked after J. Without all the people that I've worked with on Shotley ward I think my work journey would have been so different. I know that if they hadn't been so supportive, I would have taken longer off at the time and that would have been so damaging to my mental health.

I hope they all know how much I appreciate their friendship and support, not just the people I've named but every last person I've worked with on that ward. The NHS is so similar to the forces in that you need a very strange sense of humour to survive and believe me there's been many times on that ward that I've laughed so much I've cried. Although I no longer work there, I still keep in touch with a lot of them and I know that they are there for me and vice versa.

My life at present revolves around J and I'm quite happy for it to be like that. We spend my weekends off making memories whether that is days out or snuggling under a duvet watching movies. Whatever we do 99% of the time we are together although the pull of his friends is a lot more fun than mum these days but that's fine it just means he's growing up. I made that promise to him when Chris died that we would make hundreds of memories every year and that we will take photos of everything. I've kept that promise and we have so much fun together, he's like my not so little partner in crime and it's not often we spend a night apart unless I am away. When I go away for the night then J will stay with my parents, he has such an amazing bond with them both, it seems he can tell Nana things he can't tell me but he's a Grandads boy through and through. However, one weekend he stayed with my brother Ad, his wife Claire and their twin girls Emily and Grace. He had such a wonderful weekend with them and it's so nice that he has a good relationship with his cousins, although I think they may all wind each other up on purpose but that of course works both ways. Ad and Claire have been such wonderful role models for him and like dad, Ad is a great male role model. It's so important for J to see what family life can be like and with our family he has a wonderful example of that.

I love being with J and he never fails to put a smile on my face or make me laugh and I will never ever regret the time I spend with him just in the same breath I will never stop doing it whilst he wants to spend time with me. The bond we have is amazing and we can read each other so well, he knows by the slightest change in my tone how I'm feeling, and I know by one look at his face what's going on. That's a bond that will never be broken I don't believe, and I also think it's a bond that will get stronger over the years. I'm hoping that it's going to get us through the teenage years!

As the title of this chapter says though life does go on. Chris and I had been separated for 18 months when he died, I had used that time to find myself and was finally feeling ready to maybe start dating again but then I was thrown into the depths of grief. It was such a turbulent time in my mind, I was just coming out the other side of grieving for our marriage and then I was right back at the beginning again but this time it hurt even more. I dipped my toe in the dating world a couple of times, but I don't believe I was really ready to take that step I think I was just fed up with people asking me if I had met anyone. I have now met someone who makes me happy, the relationship is complicated in that we live a fair distance apart, but I've never done simple! We don't see each other as much as we would like but it ensures the time, we have is quality time. He's taught me that I can be open to being with someone again and more importantly that I'm worthy of love, the confidence that he gives me is amazing and I thank my lucky stars every day for the fact that he came into my life. We started as friends and we speak everyday about everything and anything, he is such an amazing source of support and I'm not sure where I'd be without him. I'm not sure where it's heading but I am enjoying myself and he makes me smile. For now, I am embracing it for what it is and that makes me happy.

Certain times of the year are still extremely difficult for us, mind you it's still early days in the whole grieving process. The first of everything was easily the worst but the pain of anniversary's never really gets easier, Chris's birthday, our anniversary and the anniversary of his death. Christmas will never be the same I don't think mainly because Chris always loved that time of the year and because it's so close to when he died. Also, Jamie's birthday is quite bittersweet because as much as we celebrate it and I go all out to make it a fantastic day for him there is someone missing from it. We get through them all though and really all they do is make us stronger, people say time is a great healer and with certain things that's true but that's not the case with everything.

We are looking to the future though; J is looking ahead to what he wants to do when he's older. At the moment it keeps changing but he is turning into a very talented baker, he is also toying with the idea of being a Royal Marine, whatever he chooses to I have no doubts he'll achieve it, but he'd also like to raise more money for SSAFA as well. I have managed to secure a foot on the housing ladder which has been my dream since we moved back and one, I wasn't sure that I would achieve but I have and I'm extremely proud of myself. I don't like to not achieve the targets I set myself, it also teaches Jamie that things are possible if you work hard enough for them.

My main aim in life though is to make sure Chris's death wasn't in vain, I will keep fighting to spread the word of PTSD and Veteran Suicide. Because of this I applied for a job with All Call Signs who work within Veterans Mental Health, this was possibly the best move I have ever made. I absolutely love my job, although at times it is emotionally exhausting, I really feel like I am making a difference. It's a very small team but a very close knit one, they are more than colleagues they are family. They are all really good with J as well which is so important to me, he loves his daily video calls with them. Working from home has made a massive difference to me, having been so ill with Covid I really struggled with my previous job and the lasting effects. However now I get more time with J, and I can rest if needed but actually my recovery is going a lot better since I changed jobs. I would love to go into public speaking and go round the country telling people our story and how suicide destroys so many lives, I have done a few talks now so hopefully the word is getting out there. Also, though I would like the stigma of suicide to be gone, nobody should be embarrassed by it, not the family and especially not the person having suicidal thoughts. It's so important that people realise that it doesn't make you weak to admit that you are struggling, in fact it makes you one of the strongest people. As Veterans we are so proud of our service but it's that pride that sometimes holds us back from opening up, that needs to change and quickly.

Support

It's not until something bad happens in your life that you realise how many people care about you. Some people say that they are surprised by the people that support them but what surprised me was how many people were there for us. We are so very lucky to be surrounded by so many wonderful, caring people. I still have down days and it's during these that I tend to shut myself away, these wonderful people don't let me do that. They drag me out of myself and don't force me to talk but they encourage it, just knowing that they are there is enough to get me going again. It's because these people know me so well that they know how to encourage me to pick myself up, if they tried to force me to talk, I would just go further into myself.

We have been supported by so many people over the last five years and without them we really wouldn't be where we are now. I have to say thank you for all the hugs, the kind words, the kicks up the arse and for all the times people were just normal with us. When you are going through something so horrendous then normal is heaven sent and definitely not something I'll complain about again. I always thought normal was boring but now it's an absolute God send, it's what I want, a normal safe life.

My mum and dad deserve another thank you and also my brother Ad and his wife Claire because their support of both myself and J has never once wavered, they've been there through all the lows as well as the highs. At no point have we been made to feel by them that we are being a pain or leaning on them too much. I'm sure mum and dad never expected when they became parents/grandparents that they would ever have to support their loved ones through something like this. I talk a lot about J's role models, but they are mine, through good and bad they have been there for us both and if I can be half the parent, they are then I'll have done a good job. Chris's dad John has also been a constant in our lives, even before Chris died, John didn't take sides when we separated and that will never be forgotten, the same goes for Graham and Karen as well (Chris's brother and sister-in-law).

Support comes in so many different ways, J's football coach, Dean supports J in so many ways. He's given him so much confidence on the football pitch and that had transferred into everyday life. Jamie gave 100% when he played and that's because his coach believed in him and that goes such a long way. The way Dean coaches is amazing, he concentrates on what the players have achieved and ways that they can build on that and every one of those kids has respect for him. J will never be a natural football player, but Dean gave him a chance and he earnt his place in the team. Gail, my best friend of over 30 years and Dean's wife has been absolutely amazing and everything and more that a best friend should be. She has not only shared our happy moments with us she has been there through the down days and listens to me whenever I need to offload.

Other good friends have let me know in their own ways that they are there for us both, simple things like being on the end of the phone if I want to talk. I don't open up very often about my feelings because that's the way I deal with it but to know that trusted friends are there makes a huge difference. Another way people have shown they care is to check in on us, not daily because they know me well enough to know that that's one thing that would start to shut me down. Knowing that there are people that want to listen to me is probably the one thing that encourages me to open up though.

I'm very lucky that I am surrounded by people that want to support us, that want us to succeed on our journey to help others. In fact, in a recent conversation with my best friend Gail she was encouraging me to write this book and telling me that people would want to read about our journey, so we can all blame her! I keep my circle small but every single person in that circle I would trust with my life and that I believe has been one of the reasons we've survived this. I have a huge support network on Twitter of all places, there is a fantastic group of Veterans and people connected to the force's community. The support that these people give each other is just amazing and I'm hugely proud to be part of it. All of that group get behind our fundraising whether that's buying raffle tickets, attending a charity ball or buying one of J's amazing VE Day t shirts. A truly wonderful group of people that support us both. Not everyone on there is like that though and I have been burnt by people that have tried to use not just myself but also J for their gain, we live and learn though.

If you are wanting to support someone the one thing, I would suggest is to let them know that you are there. Put no pressure on them whatsoever to talk, don't put a time scale on it, let them come to you when they are ready. Speaking from experience though it will mean the world to them that you are there, and they won't forget that - ever.

THE SOLDIERING ON AWARDS

I knew that SSAFA had nominated J for a 'Soldiering on Award', I hadn't told him not because I thought he wouldn't be recognised but because I knew how many inspirational people would have been nominated, it was my way of protecting him. Imagine my surprise when I received a phone call in early January 2019 from Kaija Larke who did the PR for the awards. She was ringing to ask permission to contact local newspapers and TV stations as J was under 16. She was very guarded as the finalists' names hadn't yet been released but she did tell me to expect an e mail and made me promise not to tell J before that. I'm not sure she realised what she was asking me, but I managed it, just, I did however tell my parents. That news was just far too big to not tell someone, and I thought I was going to burst with both pride and excitement. J had had an idea to help other Veterans and Service personnel and he was now being recognised by these very people, what an awesome sign of recognition. When I looked into the Soldiering On Awards, I realised just how big this was, these were National Awards and if the unthinkable were to happen and he won then this would be huge.

When I told J, he was a finalist he was absolutely blown away, it was one of the very few times I have seen him speechless. It was very safe to say though from the big smile on his face he was extremely happy about it and the fact that he couldn't stop talking about it. Then the media attention started, he was invited back onto Radio Suffolk with Mark Murphy and all of his team which it seems is one of J's favourite things to do. There were no dodgy comments this time thankfully although I don't think I needed to be there, Mark and J did just fine between them. We also did an interview for Anglia news which was then posted all over social media and had thousands of views. This wasn't about making J famous it was about spreading his message about speaking out and also listening if someone reaches out to you. If one person watched that interview and reached out, then it served its purpose. It was also about celebrating the fact that a 10yr old who was going through a horrendous time channelled that grief into helping others. J was also lucky enough to do an interview with the British Forces TV channel, so his message was heard all over the world. He is an absolute natural on the TV and radio unlike mum who would much rather stay in the background, that's something that I don't think I'll ever get used to.

In February all of the finalists were invited to a reception at the House of Lords, it was hard to convey to J just how huge this was until I told him that Donald Trump isn't allowed in there! He was thrilled with that explanation, in fact that was the way he described it to most people, he was going somewhere Trump wasn't allowed. The excitement was also helped by the fact that he was having 2 days off school, we've all been 10 and know just how exciting that is. He was lucky though that his school was fully supportive of this, and every staff member was proud of him and willing him on to win.

In the build up to the drink's reception the interest on social media was huge, every day I was showing J posts he had been tagged in through me. It was through all this media frenzy that we started talking to Assistance Dog Ziggy and his Hooman Richard, most days J and Ziggy would post to each other, with my supervision. In the week leading up to the event there was a daily countdown from both of them about seeing each other. Jamie fell that much in love with Ziggy that a working dog teddy had to be brought which has also been renamed Ziggy. Still to this day the teddy is pride of place on J's bed, he's hoping one day that a real dog will join it, he hasn't quite twisted my arm on that one yet though.

Their first meeting was everything J imagined it would be and I didn't actually see much of J at the drinks reception as he was always within a foot or two of his new best mates. It was also nice to finally meet Richard after all of our messages, what an honour it is to call him a friend, a truly inspirational man who does so much to help others. Although his own mental health has caused him all sorts of problems, he is still there to help others, a true hero.

We met so many people that night, every last one of them was a truly wonderful person and to be standing in the same room as them was a little overwhelming especially for J although I was also a little overwhelmed. When we first arrived, we met up with Alice Farrow from SSAFA who was going to be our host for the evening, it was lovely to see her again and to see a friendly face to boost my confidence which in turn boosted J's. Another example of how we use our bond to help each other without using words. We went through security and entered the reception room, trying to find a space to stand was tricky as there were an awful lot of people in attendance. Everyone it seemed wanted to talk to J which he found a bit overpowering to start with, he was polite throughout but shyer than I've ever seen him, grunts replaced words for a while. There was lots of nodding the head or smiling in answer to a question, it didn't stop him charming people though. He was taken off to do a radio interview for BFBS with Tim, who knows what they were chatting about off air but when he came back after that there was no stopping him!

To watch him talking to people like John Nichol, Luke Delahunty, Vicki Michelle was just wonderful, and he loved all of them. What an amazing experience for him to be able to spend the evening with such iconic people. We also had the great honour to talk to and have a photo with the last Dam buster which has pride of place in the living room, unfortunately he has since died which made it even more special. J was learning about the War at school and had just done a model of one of the dams, so he was in his element and told him all about it. We met so many wonderful people that night that if I was to name them all we would be here for hours, but they know who they are. The fact that they all treated J like an equal is testament to all of them and also to J, it was a very proud mum moment. I do however want to mention the other finalists in J's category; The War Widows Association of Great Britain, The Ripple Pond, Reading Force and Little Troopers. All of these organisations do wonderful things for the force's community, and it was an honour for J to stand alongside them. More than that though individually they were all remarkable people, what really stood out is that whoever won the others would all be pleased for them and that was the feeling throughout all of the categories. That speaks volumes about these awards, it's very much community based and that shows with every person who is short-listed.

Vicki Michelle and Carly Paoli read out the names of all the finalists and when it came to J, they said some of his story. To hear him spoken about in the way they did brought tears to my eyes, and I don't think I was the only one. He got a huge round of applause and I think it hit him then just what a huge achievement it was to get to the finals. Vicki Michelle also made reference to how dapper he looked in his 5-piece suit which brought a smile to his face, a different reaction to when I said he looked smart or asked him to put it on. He had been having far too much fun jumping on the bed in the hotel.

That evening passed far too quickly and before long it was time to leave, dragging J away from Ziggy was a task in itself. When we were waiting at the tube station to go back to the hotel another finalist approached J, shook his hand and told him what an inspiration he is. To hear those words about your child is amazing, we all think it but its tear jerking to hear it from strangers. J was definitely a little bit hyper when we got back to the room and understandably so, he eventually settled though, curled up with his mini-Ziggy, I imagine he was dreaming about the real one that night.

Life after the drink's reception went back to being as close to normal as it could. J was back to school and working hard towards his SATs and I was back to work, we had a fair few weeks to wait until the award ceremony so we kept busy making memories, it didn't half drag though.

THE AWARDS

Well, the suit was bought, my dress was bought, hair done, radio interview with Radio Suffolk done and we were on the train with my parents. My nerves were all over the place and J seemed to be taking everything in his stride, I think mum and dad were more nervous than him. My caseworker, Sue, had also met us at the train station and was travelling on the same train, although when we got to London, we were staying in three separate hotels it was nice to travel together though and I was over the moon that Sue was able to share the experience with us. She was and still is such an important part of our journey, so it was only fitting that she was there with us. We said goodbye to Sue at Liverpool Street and arranged to meet later that afternoon. Myself, J and my parents went off to the Park Plaza Hotel where J and I were staying. We showed off our room to my mum and dad, J was bouncing around like a lunatic, and I wasn't far off joining him lol. Neither of us have ever stayed in a room like it and I think it will be a fair few years before we do again! Mum and dad went off to book into their hotel which was just down the road and then came back so dad and J could go in the pool in our hotel, a ploy to try and calm J down. Mum and I went to check out the bar and have a glass of wine to settle our nerves, at £10 a glass we drank it slowly, although it was a lovely wine and if we couldn't treat ourselves today when could we?

We met dad and J back in our room and agreed to meet back in the bar at 17:30hrs after we had all gotten ready. Then the preparations started, me trying to get my dress over my hair (which I had had done earlier in the day) was hysterical to J and a struggle I don't want to have again, with a little help though I got there. J was dressed in his new suit as he had managed to outgrow his previous one in 2 months! After quite a few minutes fiddling we finally managed to get his bow tie done up, not an easy job when your hands are shaking beyond control, not that I was nervous of course. J made the final touches to his hair, using half a tube of hair gel and we were ready to go. Just before we left the room J looked me directly in the eyes, said I looked beautiful and thank you for everything. I think I just nodded at him, but I know I gave him a big hug, I'm not sure that words were needed. That set the stage for an emotional night.

When we got in the bar, we met up with the people we would be sharing a table with including Sue, Alice Farrow, James Grant and of course my parents. J had an extra surprise when Luke who used to work for SSAFA came in to wish him luck, he was thrilled to see him. We were introduced to Julie who works for SSAFA and her husband who would turn out to be J's entertainment during the awards. Of course, we also met up with Richard and Ziggy in the bar, it wouldn't have been the same if we hadn't. Unfortunately, when we reached our seats, we were the opposite side of the room to them, so we didn't see much of them afterwards. J and Ziggy had some pictures taken by my parents though before we went to the champagne reception.

Never have I ever seen so many large bottles of champagne in one place and I don't think I ever will again. J settled down on the one sofa with Grandad and a glass of orange juice and the I pad. That didn't last long though as people came to say hello, these included John Nichol, Sir Andrew Gregory (SSAFA), the toastmaster (who was awesome) and the Army Cadets with the selfie board. In fact, the toast master noticed I didn't have a glass at one point and brought over a tray, he must have known I was a Veteran! The atmosphere in the reception was electric, so many nervous people but everyone was chatting to each other, it was truly amazing to watch. After a couple of glasses of champagne (if you believe that) we went through to the Awards room to find our table.

The room was like something you'd see only in your dreams. It was easy to see how much work had gone into it and it was a fitting environment for all the finalists. The tables looked beautiful; in fact, the whole room did. There were so many people in there, but it didn't feel like you were crammed it although you could talk to other tables which was good. We sat down at our table, mum and dad were sat in between Alice and James and J and I were sat between Julie and Sue. Even after the event started people were coming over to say hi to J, it was wonderful to see the effect he had on people, and he dealt with the attention so well.

The time came for Jamie's category and as the nominations were read out there was a loud cheer for Jamie. We waited with bated breath for Carol Vorderman and JJ Chalmers to announce the winner……………. The War Widows Association of Great Britain. Wonderful worthy winners but as I looked at Jamie, I saw his face crumble. A completely understandable reaction I think after the reaction he had from people. He may have been upset but he put a smile on his face and applauded the winners, in that moment I realised my boy was now a young man. Nana came over and gave him a hug and I told him he was a winner in so many people's eyes. The people on the table next to us were telling him he had achieved more than some adults achieve and he should be so proud of himself and that seemed to console him, it was truly a wonderful thing to say.

But wait, Carol Vorderman started talking again and said there was a 2nd winner in the category and that was……………. JAMIE SMALL!! Wow I was in shock, J was in shock, I suddenly came back into the moment, and I had to give him a gentle push to get up, I don't think he could quite believe it, I felt exactly the same. As we walked past our table both James and dad patted J on the shoulder, I admit most of it is a blur of emotions, but I remember the cheering and as we stood on stage, I saw that J had a standing ovation. We were greeted on the stage by Carol and JJ which was amazing in itself and J was given his award which proved to be just that little bit too overwhelming and J broke down in tears. I'm sure you'll all agree that it was an emotion that every single one of us can I understand. I think it was because it meant so much to him and the reaction from others was enough to overwhelm anyone let alone an 11-year-old boy. Although a big cuddle off Carol Vorderman went some way to help though and I know many men who are extremely jealous. Whilst he was receiving super mum hugs he got another surprise, a signed Liverpool FC shirt which he thought was beyond awesome. The tears stopped just in time for the photos and the photographer (Rupert) managed to catch some amazing shots of us both and some not so flattering ones of me!

After we left the stage, we were taken out of the room to have photos taken and to do some interviews. It was whilst we were out there, we met fellow winner, the dog Finn who has since had Finns Law passed. An amazing achievement and such important news for all working animals. J was thrilled to meet him, not that he's a dog lover if you couldn't tell, he was even more thrilled when he saw them on BGT, he made sure we voted for them at every opportunity.

After we sat back at our table J was once again centre of attention with everyone coming to congratulate him. One amazing young man who's name we didn't get came to speak to J and said some truly lovely things to him then topped it by giving J his miniature medals. He said that J deserved them more then him, this was a true act of kindness as I know how much my own medals mean to me. I was gobsmacked by this and kept saying are you sure, I was told yes in no uncertain terms. If he is reading this the medals are in our wall unit and J insists on showing them to his friends and telling them what a hero, you are.

A very happy yet exhausted young man was taken to bed by Grandad and was apparently asleep within minutes. It's hard to describe my feelings about the night as there are no words to describe just how proud of J I am. Please do not underestimate just how proud I was, to have been recognised by the very people he wants to help is just huge. I can't thank the team at the 'soldiering on awards' enough. It didn't just stop there though they still support us, and they are an amazing bunch. It was such an emotional night and so many tears were shed and not just by us, I've never seen so many grown men with grit in their eyes, it must have been very dusty in there. It was such an amazing night and one which the memories will stay with both myself and J for a lifetime. I know that Chris will have been looking down on us that night with a huge smile on his face saying that's my boy, I also know that he would have been green with envy about the Liverpool shirt.

After what can only be described as the best night's sleep ever, I woke up to hundreds of posts and messages on social media. It was then that I truly realised what an effect J had had on people and not just those in the force's community. Others were recognising what I already knew that J truly is an amazing young man. The response to J winning was out of this world and he was most definitely still on a high. The whole experience of the Soldiering On Awards was fantastic, and I thank SSAFA for nominating Jamie.

ANTONY COTTON

On the Sunday after the Awards, we got in the car ready to start the long journey up to Manchester where we were going to be doing an interview for SSAFA with Antony Cotton from Coronation Street. We travelled up the day before so that we could get a decent night's sleep and not look like we had been up all night, SSAFA had booked us into a hotel near the location. Too be honest it was nice to have some alone time with J, life had been so hectic, so it was awesome just to chill and watch rubbish TV together. Also staying in the hotel was Lucy Walters from SSAFA who was the person to first contact me about telling our story 2 years before. This though would be our first meeting, although after the hours we had spent on the phone it was like we had always known each other, it was so nice to finally meet her though and put a face to the voice. We woke early on the Monday morning as Radio Suffolk were ringing us to talk to J about the awards the smile on his face when he was talking to them was huge, he could have spoken to them for hours and he enjoyed every second of describing the night to them. Then we met up with Lucy and some other lovely ladies from SSAFA for breakfast, I didn't eat a lot, as a huge Corrie fan I was nervous about meeting Antony, J however ate like a horse.

We drove the couple of miles to the house where we were doing the filming and were met by the cameraman that did the first photo shoot with us which put J instantly at ease, they were soon giggling away together. We had a cup of tea and chatted until Antony arrived and we all admired the beautiful house that we were privileged to be in. Antony arrived pretty much on time which surprised me to start with and when he walked in, he was so down to earth. He made J laugh within the first couple of minutes and that set the scene for the rest of the morning. I've always respected him for everything he does for not just SSAFA but for the whole force's community, but you never quite know what people will be like in the flesh. I have to admit to being a bit worried that he would be a bit of a diva, you hear so many stories about famous people but that couldn't be further from the truth. I can't speak highly enough of him he really is an amazing man.

By the end of the morning, we were both fans, J was an extremely big one though and will be talking about it for years. I am a fan of anyone that puts a smile on J's face and for someone to spend a morning making him laugh then I will always have their back. It wasn't just that though, Antony is a truly wonderful person, there's no side to him, what you see is what you get, he just wants to help others.

The reason behind the filming was such an important one though it was in preparation for the 'big brew up'. I talked with Antony about Chris and what happened which is normally something that I don't open up about completely, but he made me feel so at ease and talking to him was so natural, it's so important that you are made to feel like that because otherwise you hold back and to help others you need to be able to speak freely. To speak to someone that gets you without having been where you are is amazing and says an awful lot about that person. The only thing I can compare it with is a very good therapy session, he let me talk and spoke only when I stopped.

We then brought J into the interview, and they spoke about his fun day, the awards, what sports Jamie likes to do and about why talking is so important. A lot of the interview consisted of the two of them pulling faces at each other, laughing, taking the mickey out of each other's football team and Antony saying the word sod!!! That is the whole thinking behind the big brew up though, it's a chance for people to talk, to laugh, to cry, whatever they need to do. We touched the subject of why it's so important to talk and it really is, it can save lives. Please never forget the hugely important message behind these things, it really can save someone's life if they are able to reach out to someone.

Antony really is the perfect person to lead something like this campaign because he really cares. A lot of people say they want to help and that they care about the subject, but Antony puts so much work into it and is a great ambassador for SSAFA. He was talking about how most of his friends are serving in the Forces and that alone makes a huge difference to how he feels about this whole area. It helps him to know what others are going through as well, he has seen his friends return from tour and has known people who have given the ultimate sacrifice and that gives him such an important insight to a world not many people understand.

When we were talking to him about Chris and everything that has happened since you could see him getting choked up and I knew then just how much this meant to him. He didn't know any of us but just by hearing our story it made him emotional which to me meant he at least understood to some degree what we had all been through, are still going through. When we watched him on Lorraine talking about the launch of the 'big brew up' he was so emotional talking about J and what he's been through and that's so important for others to see how suicide affects not just J and I but others around us. I'm sure every person who watched that interview was touched in some way, and I hope it made them all think about how they can help others and that mental health isn't something to be scared off.

A couple years on and Antony hasn't disappeared from our lives, we keep in touch over social media and J especially loves that contact. We are hoping to meet up with him when he is next in the area and Antony has become another amazing male role model for J, not because of what he does for a job but because of who he is as a person. He now follows him on Instagram and loves following what he's up to and regularly tells his mates that they are friends.

Scotty's Little Soldiers

J joined Scotty's in 2019, just in time for the Christmas party in London, what an amazing experience that was. From start to finish we were made to feel like we were the priority and the amount of planning that went into that day is just mind blowing. It was a bit nerve wrecking for us both as neither of us really knew anyone, but everyone was so friendly. J was a little shy and he kept appearing by my side throughout the day but we both left there shattered but happy with some awesome memories.

Throughout lockdown the support didn't stop, and numerous activities were put on via zoom or on the Facebook page. J took part in the virtual choir which amazed me as it involved me filming him singing a complete song, not the sort of thing he'd normally do but he was determined to be involved. The final product was tear jerking, if you get a chance have a look on You Tube for it and see for yourself just how amazing these kids are. The Christmas party in 2020 was held online, I have no idea what went on as J shut himself in his room, what I do know is that it involved glitter and lots of laughter. Is there any better sound then hearing your child proper belly laugh?

We also attended the online ball, Mum and Dad joined us for this one as J was a team captain, again the planning and entertainment was second to none. J and I may have been seen doing the Tango round the living room at the end of the evening! It was so nice to see everyone smiling, laughing and joining in and of course amazing to see how much money was raised.

As things started to open up again in 2021, Scotty's were there again to ensure that we weren't short of things to do. J attended an Outward Bound residential in the Lake District which he really wanted to do but he wasn't sure about spending a week away, however he did it and loved every second. In fact, before he even got home, he was asking to do another, not bad considering, this just shows how Scotty's helps to build confidence. We went on our first Scotty's holiday in the August to Hastings, this turned out to be really good timing as the news about the withdrawal from Afghanistan had just broken. I put a ban on watching or listening to the news but ensured J knew he could discuss it if he wanted to. He was struggling because people were saying it was all for nothing, but he knew that it was Afghan that had pushed Chris to his limit. We were able to talk about it in a safe place, just the two of us with no in your face reminders which I truly believe helped J more than anything. We both had an amazing time and with the members discount it meant J could make some awesome memories.

We finished off 2021 with the Christmas party in Manchester, after what can only be described as a horrendous drive up, we were able to enjoy the weekend. Well J was like a different lad this year; I only saw him on the Friday night when I dragged him to bed! It was different for me this year as well and actually sat and chatted with a few other mums whilst the kids were running riot. We even met another family from Suffolk which shows what a small world it is. After a good night's sleep (when J finally calmed down) we were up for an early breakfast, as J is on the council, they had to leave early for the venue to make sure everything was set up right. I met him there and that was the last time I properly saw him until it was time to leave. What I did see was him laughing, joking and a smile broader than

I had seen in years. This is what Scotty's does and why it is so important, it gives the kids a chance to be themselves, they can talk about their parents if they want but they aren't judged for it. It is truly a safe place for them all.

Army Suicide Prevention Video

I received a text message from Rupert who was the official photographer at the Soldiering on Awards, he was now working for the Army media team. He told me that he had been asked to put something together for suicide prevention day and the first people he thought of were myself and J. He then asked if we would like to be involved, I said that I would talk to J as it had to be his choice, he was 11 now and old enough to decide if he wanted to do things, especially something like this which I knew could be quite emotional. When I mentioned it to J I didn't know what he would say, this meant opening up on camera and for it to be shown on social media. Yet again that brave young man of mine surprised me, he jumped at the chance, it did help that it was Rupert that had asked, it would make a huge difference that someone he trusted would be on the other side of the camera.

After lots of messages we set on a date when I wasn't in work and J wasn't at school and also when Rupert and his team could make it, that proved to be trickier than you can imagine. They arrived in the morning bringing brew kit and donuts, I didn't expect anything else from the Army and it was an extremely good way to impress J. Thankfully J instantly fell into a relaxed relationship with them all and whilst I was talking to Rowena who would be asking the questions, J was outside being filmed playing football. I told Rowena that she could ask me anything, but we would have to play it by ear with J and if he got upset then he would need a break. Of course, she was totally onboard with this, it wasn't about causing J pain but giving him the chance to have a voice. I felt completely at ease that J was the priority in this situation and that his needs were the most important thing, if he was uncomfortable then we would stop.

They interviewed me first which was difficult because J had stayed in the kitchen where we were filming. I saw him out of the corner of my eye walk out halfway through and Rupert checked he was OK. It was a lot easier to talk without him looking at me as I didn't want to say anything that upset him. He wasn't upset though; he was just trying to compose himself before his turn. Although that said I had always shielded him before, and he had never really heard me speaking out about Chris so it must have been strange for him to hear me talking so openly. Talking about how we felt immediately after Chris died was easier than I thought, maybe because I knew the film would be used to help others, that has always been what my journey has been about, helping others. It's important that people realise what a devastating affect suicide has on those left behind, how it changes their lives forever and not just their lives but who they are as a person. That's not to say it wasn't emotional though but not as emotional as what was to come, I knew that J would go one of two ways, he would either be quite closed, or he would bare his soul. Soon enough it was J's turn to be interviewed, I was worried about how this was going to affect him, although he had spoken out about his dad before I knew this was going to be different, although I had complete trust in the team.

I stayed in the room whilst he was being filmed, not to put him off, not to check what he was saying but so he knew I was there for him, like everything else we did this as a team. When he started to talk, I hardly recognised him, he spoke with such maturity, passion and it was completely from the heart, remember J was only 11 at this point but he spoke like an adult. At one point he started to get upset and if you've seen the film, you'll know when I'm talking about, everyone in the room had tears in their eyes at that point and I knew he was close to breaking point. We took a break and within a few minutes J said he wanted to continue, a sign of his bravery and passion right there. I asked a few times if he was sure he wanted to continue and he insisted that he did, I had to follow his lead on this and trust that he wasn't pushing himself over his limits. The things he spoke about could defrost the most frozen of hearts, he was straight to the point, no beating around the bush and I knew he would hit people right in the heart. I knew then that the final film would be powerful, I didn't realise just how powerful though. Although J was 11 at the time he spoke with a maturity way beyond his young years, when he looked into the camera you couldn't escape either the pain or love in his eyes, it was like you were looking right into his soul. I was so proud watching him and didn't realise until he asked me if I was alright that tears were rolling down my face, that exact moment tells you exactly how much he cares about other people. I know I use the word proud a lot but it's true and there's no other way to describe it, he's such an amazing young man and I hope I've conveyed that.

Rowena sent me the final edit the day before it was going live, I was flabbergasted by it, it was the most powerful short film I'd ever seen, and I knew it was going to have a huge impact. I couldn't show anyone before it went live and that was so hard because I was so proud of what we had both achieved, I did show J though and he had the same response – tears. If it could reduce us to tears and it's our story just, what affect would it have on others? I was both excited and nervous about it going live the next day, how were others going to receive it, would we get good or bad comments? We had really put ourselves out there and we were totally at ease with what we had done but social media can be a very cruel place. I wasn't worried about me, people can say what they want but I was worried about J, if people disagreed with it would it stop him from opening up again?

It didn't take long to find out, the film had a huge impact on social media and had thousands of shares and hundreds of thousands of views. I struggled to keep up with all the comments and shares, but I tried to acknowledge everyone that had reacted to it, that proved to be extremely hard though and I apologise to those I missed. J told his English teacher what he had done, and she googled it and showed it to the class, he got such a wonderful reaction from his friends which is just amazing. A big thank you to his teacher as well because the reaction she gave to J really put a smile on his face and made him feel so proud. I still share that film today and I will continue to share it because people need to be aware of our story and suicide prevention is not just one day of the year it should be every day. I've received so many messages about that film and know that we have saved more than one life by doing it. Those messages make me emotional, not because I'm sad but because we have saved a family from going through the pain we are and that was exactly why we did it. The film also made people look at their own lives as well, they looked at their kids and imagined what pain they would go through and that gave them the push to get help. This was what we wanted more than anything, for people to reach out and realise there's no shame in that, not only that, someone who asks for help is the bravest person around and more people need to realise that.

Life Today

On Remembrance Day in '19 and '21 I marched alongside other Veterans on behalf of SSAFA at the Cenotaph which was a huge honour and something I have wanted to do for years. I saw people over both those weekends that I've not seen in years and made lots of new friends, hopefully I will be doing it this year as well. Along the way of our journey, I did a talk for the Project Nova team who do amazing work with Veterans, and I really enjoyed that experience and what I was saying seemed to go down well and hit home. I have also done a podcast with Ren Kapur MBE who is part of the Soldiering On team and Hugh Keir who are both now friends. Doing things like this mean although I'm out of my comfort zone our story is still getting out there.

J is still fundraising, he did a design for VE Day for a SSAFA competition, and we had it made into a t shirt, he raised over £1300 that also included the auction of the original picture. Yet another awesome achievement and one that he is very proud of. I travelled to London at the beginning of March '20 and met with the Veterans Minister Johnny Mercer to tell him our story. That was an experience and a half, and I know a lot of people aren't a fan of him, but I was thoroughly impressed. He made me feel extremely at ease and I wasn't rushed or made to feel he wasn't interested, there's a lot of work going on in the background we just need to be patient. I held a ball in March just before the lockdown started and that raised a further £6000 for SSAFA, it was a lot of work but extremely worth it. We didn't sell as many tickets as we wanted but with the impending lock down that wasn't a surprise. I think everyone enjoyed themselves though and it encouraged me to organise another one in September 21 which raised over £7000.

During lockdown J did an interview over zoom with Johnny Mercer, he asked a full range of questions ranging from his dad – women in the forces – would Boris Johnson be his friend! A fair bit of time was spent discussing who would win in a game of table tennis as well, J is insistent that he would win so we will see. For the Minister to take time out of his hectic life was great and an experience that J really enjoyed. I also did an interview with BFBS on behalf of The Ripple Pond, they are an amazing charity that give support to forces families that care for someone with PTSD.

So, as you can see, we are keeping ourselves busy, still fundraising and still trying to raise awareness about mental health. This is our life now; it may not be the life we once knew but it's a good life and in a lot of ways I consider us lucky. Our journey is full of lots of positives but please don't think they have come easy to us; they have come about because J used the worst experience of his life to help others. We will never ever forget Chris, he will always be J's dad and because of that he will always be with us, he lives on through J.

I hope you have enjoyed sharing our journey, please continue to support us because this is nowhere near the end. Continue to share our message that a person who asks for help is not weak, they are in fact extremely strong.

WE CAN'T CHANGE WHAT HAS HAPPENED TO US,

BUT,

WE CAN HELP TO CHANGE IT FOR OTHERS

Acknowledgements

There are so many people that have helped and supported us through our journey and if I were to mention them all it would go on for pages. We would like to thank you to each and every one of you from the bottom of our hearts but below is a list of people that deserve a special thank you.

Mum and Dad

My brother Adrian and his wife Claire

Chris's dad John

Chris's brother Graham and his wife Karen

Gail Barker and her husband Dean

Sharon, Gaz, Iain (and the rest of our Twitter family)

My colleagues/friends at All Call Signs

Gill Cannone

Vicki Bisset

Sue Cross

SSAFA head office

Anthony Cotton

Johnny Mercer

Scotty's Little Soldiers

Hidden Warriors CIC

Soldiering On Team

The Ripple Pond

Project Nova

This list is by no means exhaustive.

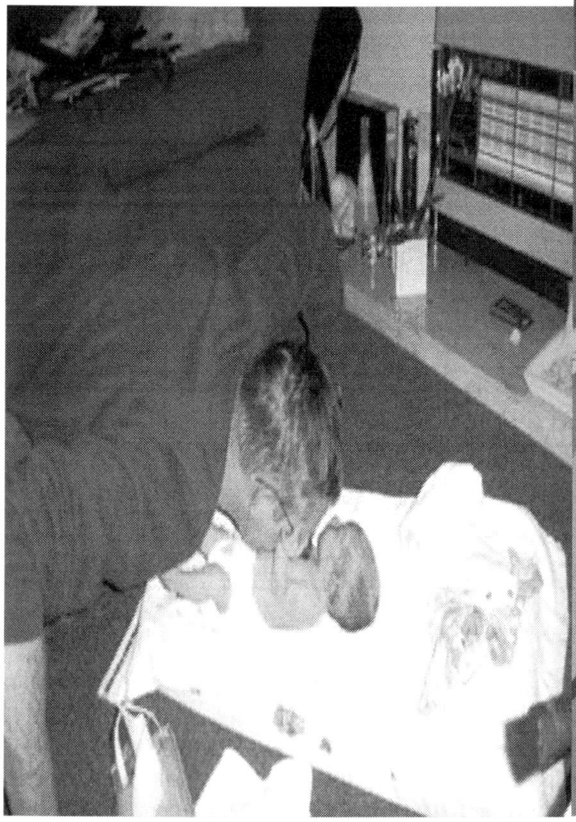
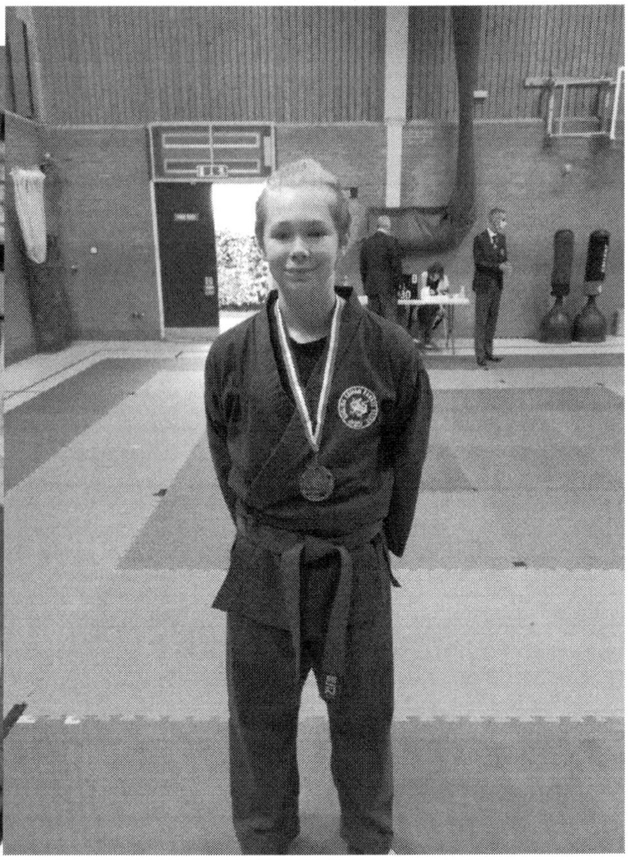
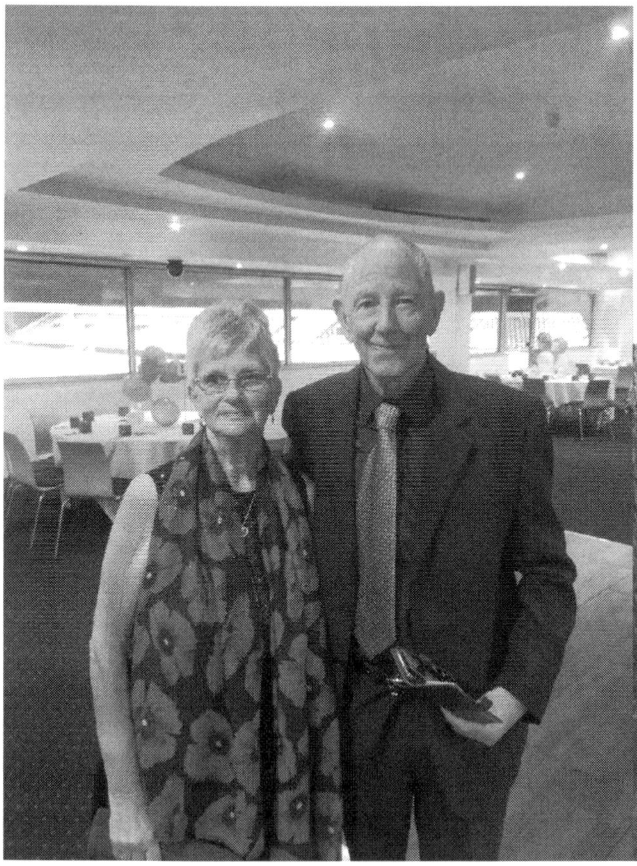
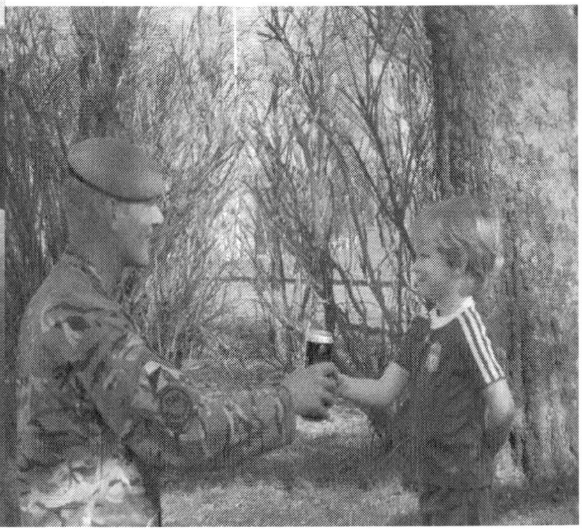

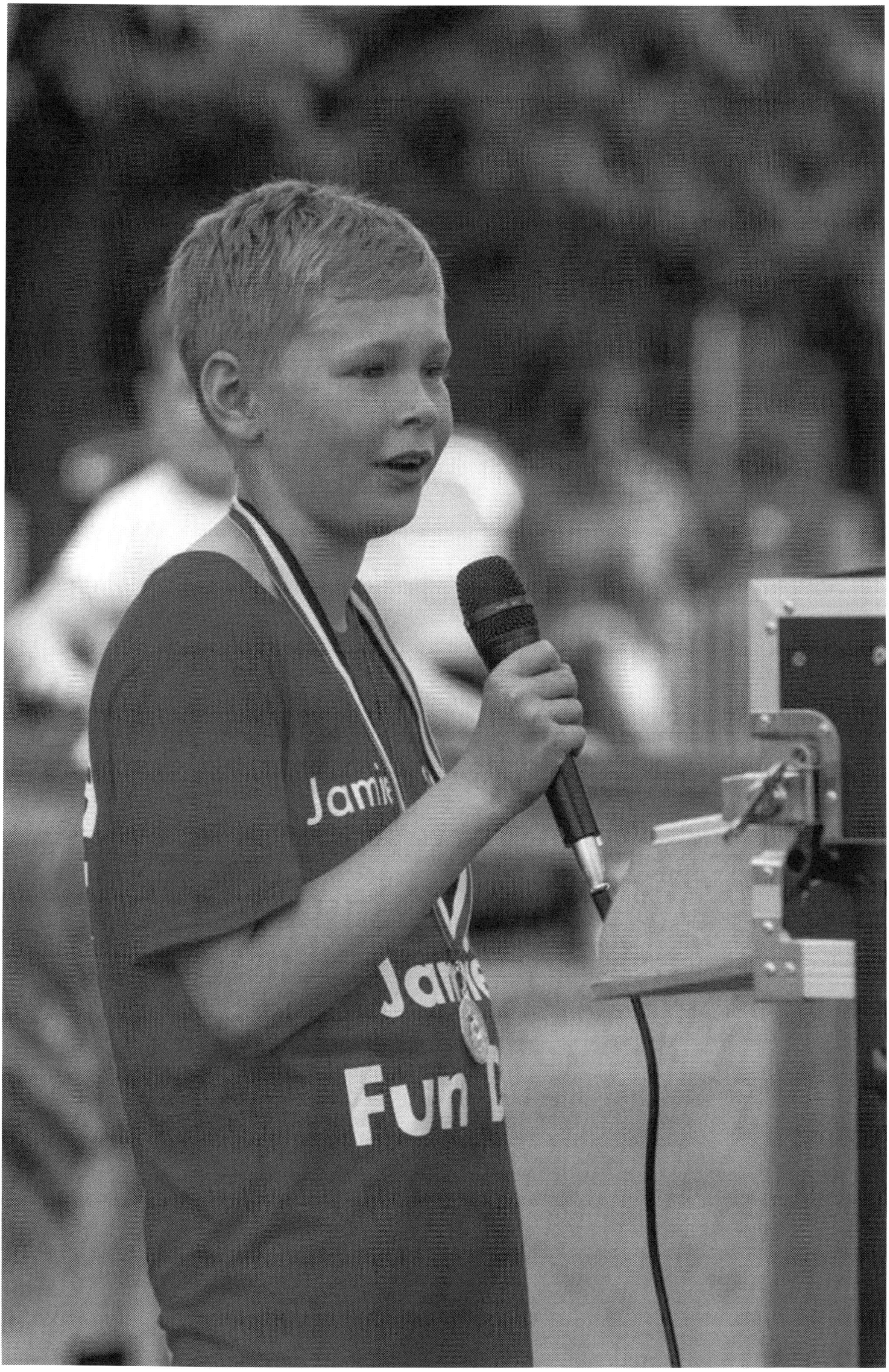

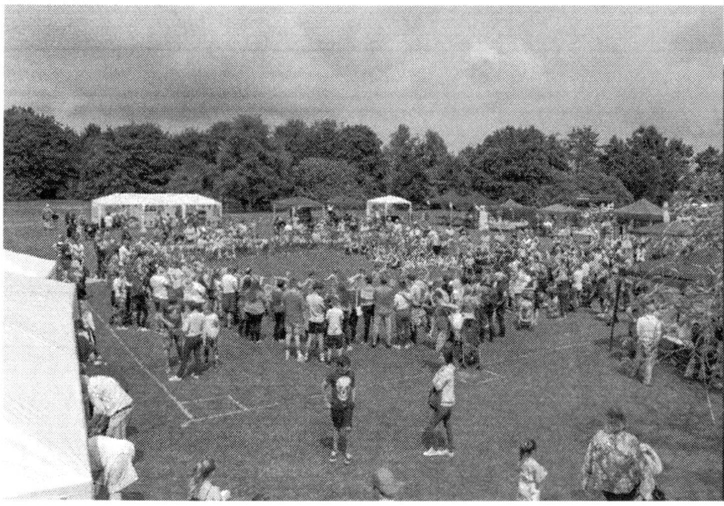

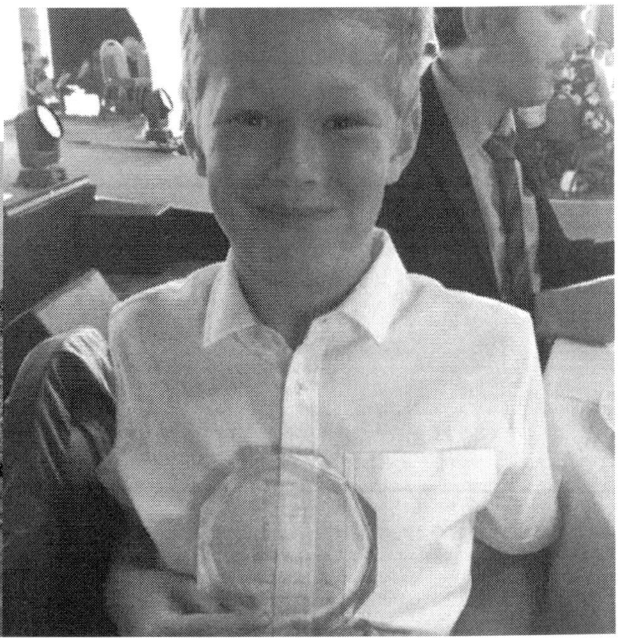

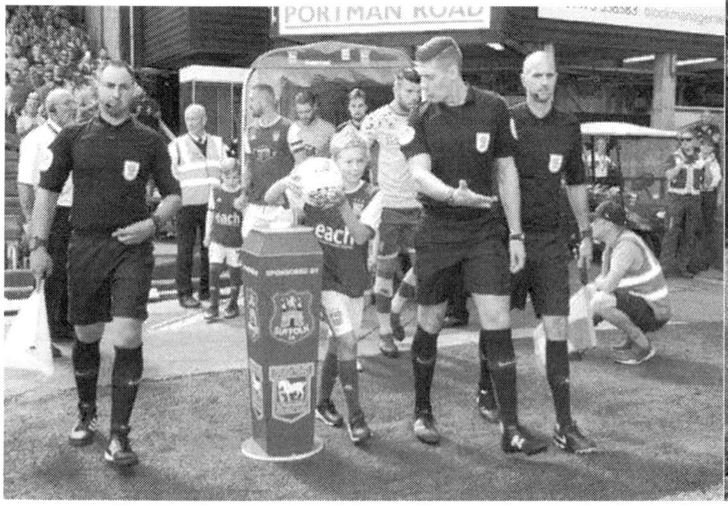
PORTMAN ROAD

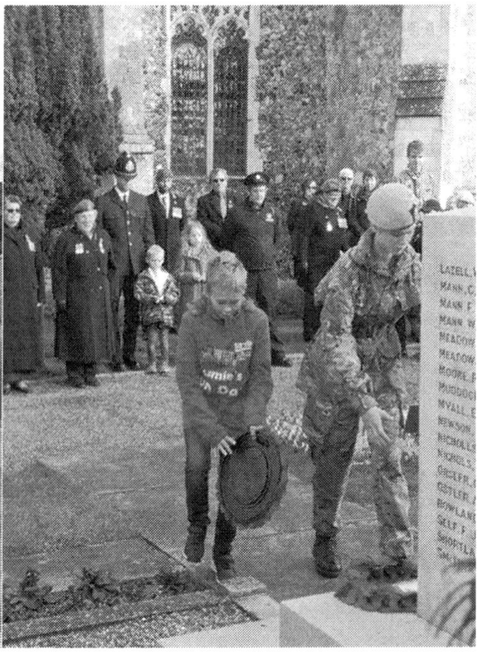

CAPITA
GREENWICH HOSPITAL
CISCO
SPECTRA
London Stock Exchange Group
REDWOOD

02/08/2018

LEFT LANE

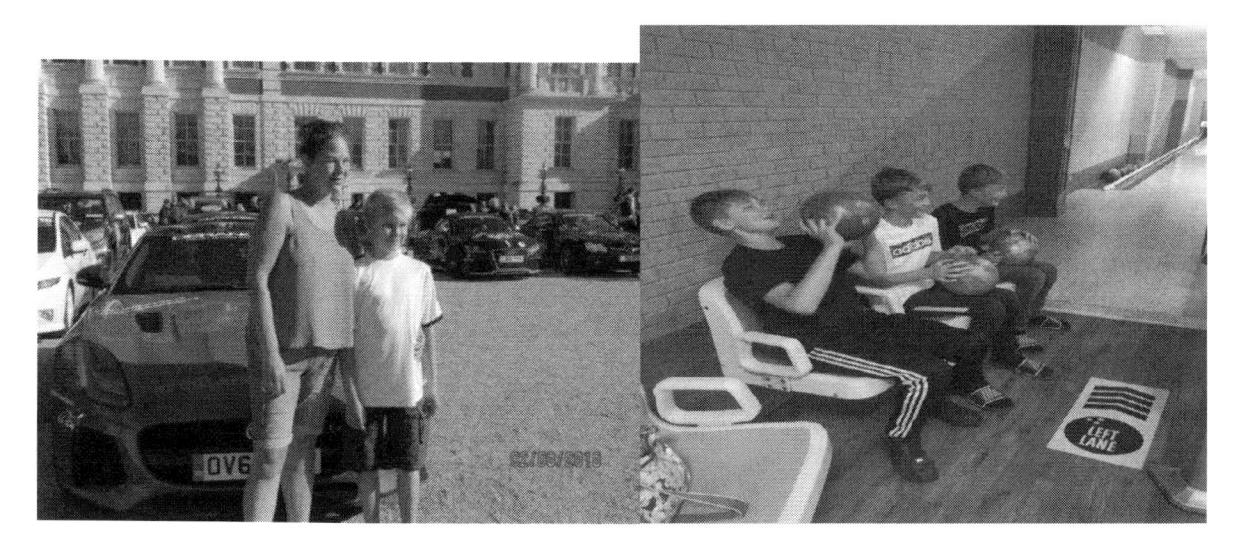

Printed in Great Britain
by Amazon